Cambridge Elements

Elements in the Philosophy of Immanuel Kant
edited by
Desmond Hogan
Princeton University
Howard Williams
University of Cardiff
Allen Wood
Indiana University

KANT ON RATIONAL SYMPATHY

Benjamin Vilhauer
City University of New York, City College and Graduate Center

Shaftesbury Road, Cambridge CB2 8EA, United Kingdom

One Liberty Plaza, 20th Floor, New York, NY 10006, USA

477 Williamstown Road, Port Melbourne, VIC 3207, Australia

314–321, 3rd Floor, Plot 3, Splendor Forum, Jasola District Centre, New Delhi – 110025, India

103 Penang Road, #05–06/07, Visioncrest Commercial, Singapore 238467

Cambridge University Press is part of Cambridge University Press & Assessment, a department of the University of Cambridge.

We share the University's mission to contribute to society through the pursuit of education, learning and research at the highest international levels of excellence.

www.cambridge.org
Information on this title: www.cambridge.org/9781009486606

DOI: 10.1017/9781009371193

© Benjamin Vilhauer 2024

This publication is in copyright. Subject to statutory exception and to the provisions of relevant collective licensing agreements, no reproduction of any part may take place without the written permission of Cambridge University Press & Assessment.

When citing this work, please include a reference to the DOI 10.1017/9781009371193

First published 2024

A catalogue record for this publication is available from the British Library.

ISBN 978-1-009-48660-6 Hardback
ISBN 978-1-009-37117-9 Paperback
ISSN 2397-9461 (online)
ISSN 2514-3824 (print)

Cambridge University Press & Assessment has no responsibility for the persistence or accuracy of URLs for external or third-party internet websites referred to in this publication and does not guarantee that any content on such websites is, or will remain, accurate or appropriate.

Kant on Rational Sympathy

Elements in the Philosophy of Immanuel Kant

DOI: 10.1017/9781009371193
First published online: December 2024

Benjamin Vilhauer
City University of New York, City College and Graduate Center
Author for correspondence: Benjamin Vilhauer, bvilhauer@ccny.cuny.edu

Abstract: This Element explains Kant's distinction between rational sympathy and natural sympathy. Rational sympathy is regulated by practical reason and is necessary for adopting as our own those ends of others which are contingent from the perspective of practical rationality. Natural sympathy is passive and can prompt affect and dispose us to act wrongly. Sympathy is a function of a posteriori productive imagination. In rational sympathy, we freely use the imagination to step into others' first-person perspectives and associate imagined intuitional contents with the concepts others use to communicate their feelings. This prompts feelings in us that are like their feelings.

Keywords: Kant, sympathy, empathy, imagination, first-person perspective, communication, aesthetic ideas, friendship, sage, imperfect duty

© Benjamin Vilhauer 2024

ISBNs: 9781009486606 (HB), 9781009371179 (PB), 9781009371193 (OC)
ISSNs: 2397-9461 (online), 2514-3824 (print)

Contents

1 Introduction   1

2 The Distinction Between Rational and Natural Sympathy   4

3 A Debate about Translating *Doctrine of Virtue* §§34–5, and a Concern about Passivity   10

4 Sympathy and the Imagination   13

5 Putting Ourselves in Others' Places   20

6 Correctly Communicating Feeling   23

7 What Problem in Kant's Ethics Is Solved by Rational Sympathy?   27

8 Responding to Exclusionists, and Distinguishing Adopting and Promoting Ends   30

9 How Rational Sympathy Allows Adoption of Merely Permissible Ends   33

10 Sages and Sympathy in Kant's Theory of Friendship   38

11 Friendship as an Ideal of Sharing All Our Ends and All Our Feelings   42

12 Four Objections to the Rationally Sympathetic Interpretation of Friendship   46

13 Sympathy as a Moral Incentive, and Its Relationship to Respect   50

14 Contemporary and Historical Connections to Empathy   54

15 Conclusion   57

    List of Abbreviations   59

    Bibliography   61

1 Introduction

In the *Groundwork of the Metaphysics of Morals* (1785), Immanuel Kant tells a famous and infamous story about a philanthropist whose benevolent actions only have "genuine moral worth" when his "sympathetic participation [*Theilnehmung*] in the fate of others" has been "extinguished" by "grief," and he acts "simply from duty" (G 4:398). The natural reading of the grieving philanthropist is that he is motivated only by the feeling of respect for the moral law, since Kant emphasizes two pages later that "*duty is the necessity of an action from respect for law*" (G 4:400). Kant says that while it is "amiable" to be "sympathetically attuned [*theilnehmend gestimmte*]," it is "on the same footing with other inclinations," and we can have a "far higher worth than what a mere good-natured temperament" would impart "even if we are cold and indifferent to the sufferings of others" (G 4:398).[1]

Kant's emphasis on the claim that dutiful yet cold and indifferent agents can have a far higher worth than sympathetic agents has long prompted criticism, famously including these snarky verses from Kant's contemporary Friedrich Schiller:

> Gladly I serve my friends, but alas I do it with pleasure
> Hence I am plagued with doubt that I am not a virtuous person.
>
> Sure, your only resource is to try to despise them entirely,
> And then with aversion to do what your duty enjoins you.[2]

Schiller's remarks are not a fair representation of what Kant says in the *Groundwork*, since Kant does not even appear to suggest that we should avoid sympathy or cultivate antipathy. Kant's point is that in the grieving philanthropist case, "the worth of character comes out" (G 4:398–9). But the *Groundwork* can indeed seem to claim that agents without sympathy can be motivated by respect for law alone to do everything that matters for morality. The *Critique of Practical Reason*, published just a few years later (1788), can seem to reinforce this *Groundwork* theme. There Kant writes that "[r]espect for the moral law is ... the sole moral incentive" (CPrR 5:78, also see 5:81), and that "sympathetic benevolence" is not "the genuine moral maxim of our conduct" (CPrR 5:82, also see 5:85). These remarks have prompted many to object that Kant's ethics is too emotionally detached to properly value feelings essential to important kinds of interpersonal connections.[3]

---

[1] The interpretation presented in this Element draws on and supplements the same overall approach that was first developed in Vilhauer 2021a, 2021b and 2022.
[2] *Über die Grundlage der Moral*, trans. A.B. Bullock, quoted in Paton (1948: 48).
[3] Allen Wood is not a proponent of this objection, but see (1999: 28) for helpful discussion. Carol Hay (2013: 56–62) calls this the "emotions objection." Helga Varden discusses it as a part of the "universal formalism" objection (2020a: 9–31, 165–185).

Kant's later book, *The Metaphysics of Morals* (1797), received significantly less scholarly attention than the *Groundwork* and second *Critique* for many decades, even though it is the book for which the *Groundwork* was meant to provide the foundation. In *The Metaphysics of Morals,* Kant paints an apparently quite different picture of sympathy: He tells us that "active sympathetic participation [*thätige Theilnehmung*] in [others'] fate is a duty," and that "compassion [*Mitgefühl*]" is "one of the drives that Nature has implanted in us to do what the representation of duty alone would not accomplish'" (MM 6: 457). Here, though his terms are not quite the same, he tells us that morality requires us to sympathize, and that sympathy allows us to do something morally important which respect for law (the representation of duty) alone cannot motivate us to do. This implies that respect for law is not sufficient for morality.

Many insightful scholars have addressed the *Metaphysics of Morals* and its remarks on sympathy in recent decades, and this book builds upon their work. Two strategies available to interpreters seeking to integrate these passages into a consistent view might be called "exclusion" and "inclusion." Exclusion aims at explaining the larger role for sympathy in the *Metaphysics of Morals* than appears to be allowed in the *Groundwork* by housing sympathy in parts of moral deliberation and motivation which are external to the activity of autonomous willing. The goal of exclusion is to show that even in the *Metaphysics of Morals*, sympathy is *not* strictly speaking *necessary*, and the essential moral motivation is still being performed by respect for law, to ensure that Kant is not read as encouraging "impurity," that is, encouraging the dependence of our wills upon incentives other than the law alone to do our duty (Rel 6:30).[4] By contrast, inclusion seeks to make sympathy *part* of the activity of the autonomous will, in

---

[4] Marcia Baron raises this concern about impurity (1995: 218). I take Baron, Ann Margaret Baxley, Barbara Herman, Carl Hildebrand, Tyler Paytas, Nancy Sherman, and Jens Timmermann to offer exclusion interpretations. Baxley and Sherman hold that Kant *could* endorse what I call inclusion, though they think he does not actually do so (Baxley 2010: 168; Sherman 1997: 150). Baron, Herman, Hildebrand, and Sherman all see Kantian sympathy as primarily making an epistemic contribution to practical reasoning. Baron and Sherman think sympathy directs our attention to situations in which we can help (Baron 1995: 220; Sherman 1997: 146). Herman recognizes that Kant distinguishes between two ways of sympathizing (1993: 17) but sees sympathy as at best accidentally related to morality (1993: 5) though she acknowledges that sympathetic feeling may be necessary for learning what she calls "rules of moral salience" (1993: 82). Hildebrand argues that Kantian sympathy does not entail sympathetic feeling – it is primarily a cognitive virtue which helps us better understand how to contribute to others' well-being, and sympathetic feeling may be helpful but is not necessary (Hildebrand 2023: 975–976). Paytas argues that sympathy is important because moral patients' needs for emotional connection are such that agents often cannot succeed in helping them without sympathy (Paytas 2015: 363–368). Timmermann (n.d.) argues that the proper role of sympathy is not to cause beneficent action, but rather to initiate beneficence from respect by prompting us to think about whether we should act.

a way that demonstrates that no impurity is involved, so that sympathy can have standing as a moral incentive alongside respect.[5]

This Element is intended to contribute to inclusion. It argues that Kant distinguishes between two ways of sympathizing. The first is passive and driven by instinct or inclination, and is labeled *natural* sympathy, taking a cue from the *Metaphysics of Morals*, where Kant says that it "spreads naturally [*natürlicher Weise*]" (MM 6:457). The second is active and guided by practical reason, and labeled *rational* sympathy, taking a cue from Friedländer's Anthropology notes, where Kant refers to it as "reason's sympathy [*Antheil der Vernunft*]" (Anth-F 25:610). Kantian sympathy is a function of a posteriori productive imagination. In rational sympathy we draw on the imagination's voluntary powers to subjectively unify the contents of intuition, in order to imaginatively put ourselves in others' places, and to associate imagined intuitional contents with the concepts others use to convey their feelings, so that those contents prompt feelings in us that are like their feelings.

The theory of rational sympathy solves a problem about how we can voluntarily fulfill our imperfect duty to adopt, rather than merely promote, others' *merely permissible ends* (MPEs), that is, the ends which together constitute their end of happiness, and have value only because they have been set by rational agents. Others' MPEs are individuated in terms of their own concepts of their MPEs, and we can only adopt their MPEs in terms of their concepts, since to adopt them in terms of different concepts would be to adopt different ends. Others' concepts of their MPEs typically (perhaps always) contain marks of the first person, and should contain no marks of law except permissibility. Rational sympathy allows us to adopt ends individuated in terms of concepts with such marks because rational sympathy allows us to voluntarily adopt others' first-person perspectives in imagination, and to voluntarily shape our contingent feelings so that such concepts motivate us despite their underdetermination by law.

The theory of rational sympathy also solves an interpretative puzzle in Kant's theory of friendship. Kant sometimes presents his ideal of virtue in the form of a figure he calls the *sage*, who is not a "finite *holy* [being] (who could never be tempted to violate duty)," but rather a human being who has "*autocracy* of

---

[5] I take Lara Denis, Melissa Seymour Fahmy, Paul Guyer, and Allen Wood to offer inclusion interpretations. Wood argues that in "Kant's own terms," the grieving philanthropist's motive "would be much more plausibly regarded as 'love of human beings'" (Wood 2008: 35), and sympathy is naturally understood as an aspect of such love. Guyer describes the grieving philanthropist scenario as a "thought experiment" (Guyer 2010: 148) – his view seems to be that it is possible as a matter of practical rationality that the grieving philanthropist could be motivated by respect alone, but human psychology is such that we must be motivated by sympathy to act beneficently. According to this book, it is not possible even as a matter of practical rationality to take others' subjective ends as our own without sympathy. The views of Denis and Fahmy are discussed in detail below.

practical reason," that is, mastery of "one's inclinations when they rebel against the law" (MM 6:383). Kant thinks the sage represents an ideal to which we should all aspire. The sage can appear to reject sympathetic suffering when she cannot help a suffering friend. This has contributed to the force of the detachment objection. The theory of rational sympathy shows that this appearance is mistaken. Sages as well as ordinary people should suffer with friends even when they cannot help, since we ought to take friends' MPEs as our own, and sympathy is necessary to adopt friends' MPEs.

Kant's theory of sympathy accords not only with everyday phenomenology but also with contemporary empirical psychology. His distinction between rational sympathy and episodes of natural sympathy which prompt the agency-disrupting feelings Kant calls *affects* is similar, and plausibly identical, to a distinction drawn in contemporary empirical psychology between *empathic concern* and *empathic distress*. The relationship between Kantian sympathy and the contemporary understanding of empathy highlights an interesting historical connection. Johann Gottfried von Herder has been claimed to be the originator of the contemporary concept of empathy. However, Kant's influence on Herder while Herder was developing his ideas about empathy suggests that Kant too may have played an important role in originating the contemporary concept of empathy.

2 The Distinction Between Rational and Natural Sympathy

Kant draws an explicit distinction between the two ways of sympathizing which this Element labels rational and natural sympathy in five texts, ranging over twenty years: the Friedländer Anthropology lecture notes (1775–6); the Mrongovius Anthropology lecture notes (1784–5); the Vigilantius Ethics lecture notes (1793–4); *The Metaphysics of Morals* (1797); and *Anthropology from a Pragmatic Point of View* (1798).[6] Kant describes the distinction with varied terminology, but the same distinction can be discerned in all five texts. It is only Kant's eliding or obscuring of the distinction in the *Groundwork* and *Critique of Practical Reason* that produces the tension described in the introduction. This section describes the distinction with quotes from the five texts, drawing on additional texts to explain key concepts. The rational side of the distinction is labeled with "(a)" and the natural side with "(b)."[7]

---

[6] Many Kant passages in this book are drawn from lecture notes taken by students or professional note-takers. These notes must be considered less authoritative than Kant's published works. But the notes typically correspond closely to Kant's published remarks, and they often augment Kant's published remarks in ways that add depth and detail, so they are nonetheless crucial sources.

[7] For previous discussions of these passages which are illuminating despite not drawing the global distinction between rational and natural sympathy presented here, see for example, Baron (1995), Baxley (2010), Denis (2000), Fahmy (2009), Guyer (2010), Paytas (2015), Sherman (1997), Timmermann (2016), and Wood (1999, 2008).

2.1 Text 1: Anthropology Friedländer, 1775–6

The Friedländer Anthropology distinguishes (a) "reason's sympathy [*Antheil der Vernunft*]" (Anth-F 25:610), and (b) "physical sympathy [*physicalischen Sympathie*]" (Anth-F 25:607). Reason's sympathy is experienced "in accordance with ideas" (Anth-F 25:607). Physical sympathy is "based not on deliberation, but on animality" (Anth-F 25:607). Kant thinks of animality as part of human nature (CPrR 5:127 n, MM 6:420). He does not see it as a source of evil in the way some ethical traditions do – he sees what he calls the "predisposition to animality" as a "predisposition to the good" (Rel 6:26–8). However, animality must be regulated by practical reason to be integrated into the ethical life.[8] Kant says that "as soon as I am not the master" of physical sympathy, "but am placed in it against my will, then it is an affect [*Affect*]" (Anth-F 25:611). *Affect* is a technical term in Kant's moral psychology that he uses throughout his practical philosophy. Affect refers to feeling that we allow to develop without moderation by reason, and which can thus be sudden and overwhelming in a way that is damaging to agency. Affect "makes reflection ... impossible or more difficult" (MM 6:407), and sympathy [*Antheil*] can "rise into an affect, or rather degenerate into it" (MM 6:409). Affect can prevent us from helping others effectively even when we discover means to do so (Anth 7:253, Anth-F 25:589). It can also dispose us to act wrongly when it conflicts with duty, as in Barbara Herman's example of an onlooker moved by sympathy to help a thief having difficulty moving his loot (Herman 1993: 4–5). Kant gives the example of a judge whose "sympathy becomes an affect" and fails to hand down a just sentence (Anth-F 25:611, also see Rel 6:30). The Friedländer Anthropology defines affect as "[t]hat degree of sensation that makes us unable to estimate and compare the object with the sum total of all our sensation": One example is "joy ... if one is pleased with an object which has no noticeable influence on the whole of our well-being"; another is "if one becomes angry about a dish having been broken in two," which Kant says likewise has no noticeable impact on our well-being as a whole (Anth-F 25:589). This suggests that one way sympathetic affect can prompt error is by causing us to arbitrarily focus on particular features of others' experience in ways that exaggerate their impact on their happiness as a whole and diminish the accuracy of our sympathy.

2.2 Text 2: Anthropology Mrongovius, 1784–5

The same distinction between rational and natural sympathy, or perhaps a somewhat more general distinction that includes this distinction as a species, is drawn in the Mrongovius Anthropology. These are notes on Kant's lectures

---

[8] Physical sympathy is also related to animality in that nonhuman animals sympathize too: "when a pig is butchered, then the others scream" (Anth-F 25:576).

during the 1784/5 winter term, demonstrating that Kant was lecturing on the distinction at the beginning of the year the *Groundwork* was published (1785). Here, Kant draws the distinction in the terms (a) "sensitivity [*Empfindsamkeit*]" and (b) "sentimentality[t] [*Empfindelei*]" (Anth-Mr 25:1320–1), which is also called "touchiness [*Empfindlichkeit*]" at Anth-Mr 25:1320. Sensitivity "is the faculty of being able to have a sensation of the agreeable and disagreeable," and a "strength" which allows us to "choose for others what they will enjoy" (ibid.). It "does not come from the senses, but from concepts" (Anth-Mr 25:1320). Sentimentality, on the other hand, is a "weakness" that makes it possible to be "easily carried away by every sensation" and prevents "rational reflection" (Anth-Mr 25:1320–1). The relationship between *Empfindsamkeit*/*Empfindelei* and sympathy may not be entirely perspicuous here, but it is suggested by Kant's idea that *Empfindsamkeit* is a capacity of feeling that allows us to choose for others what they will enjoy. Conclusive evidence of the connection is provided in Kant's discussion of the *Empfindsamkeit*/*Empfindelei* distinction in *Anthropology from a Pragmatic Point of View* (text 5 below).

2.3 Text 3: Vigilantius Ethics, 1793–4

The Vigilantius Ethics notes date from 1793–4, just a few years prior to the publication of the *Metaphysics of Morals*. These notes include a discussion of communication in friendship which distinguishes (a) "moral" sympathy and (b) "instinctual" sympathy:

> [Friends] ... communicate not only their feelings and sensations to one another, but also their thoughts ... [T]he mutual disclosure of thoughts is ... the ground for the communication of feeling ... we must have an idea of the feeling in advance, and must hence have employed reason, in order to have known it accurately [*genau*] before we communicate [t] it [*ehe wir sie mitteilen*], so that the feeling thereafter may be correct [*richtig*] and not instinctual; without thoughts, therefore, we would have no feelings, at least none of a moral kind; the other would be able to express[t] [*äußern*] not moral, but only instinctual fellow-feeling (sympathy). (Eth-V 27:677)

Here Kant claims that there is a way to establish (a) moral rather than (b) instinctual sympathy between people. It turns on *reasoning* about one's feelings so that one can think *accurately* about them, and then communicating the feeling so that the "feeling thereafter may be correct" – in other words, communicating the feeling so that the sympathizer can correctly sympathize. I take Kant's view in this passage to be that correct sympathy is not only accurate, in that it involves feelings like the other's feelings, but also moral, in that it moderates sympathy to prevent affect and avoids sympathy that disposes us to act wrongly. Kant characterizes instinctual sympathy only indirectly in this passage, implying that it is not mediated by thinking and reasoning in the same way or to the same degree as moral sympathy, and does not afford the same possibility of correct sympathy. The conceptual connections between animality and instinct (OFBS 2:27, CPrR 5:127, Anth 7:197, and Ped 9:443) link this discussion to the Friedländer discussion (Anth-F 25:607), providing evidence that Kant is exploring the same distinction.[9]

2.4 Text 4: *The Metaphysics of Morals*, 1797

The most famous passage addressing the distinction between rational and natural sympathy is *Doctrine of Virtue* §§34–5 in the *Metaphysics of Morals*, entitled "Sympathetic Feeling Is Generally a Duty" in the Cambridge translation (MM 6:456–8). Here, Kant distinguishes (a) *"humanitas practica,"* the *"capacity* and the *will* to *share in others' feelings [Gefühle mitzuteilen],"* which is *"free,"* and based on "practical reason," and to which "[t]here is [an] obligation," and (b) *"humanitas aesthetica,"* "the receptivity, given by nature itself, to the feeling of joy and sadness in common with others," which is *"unfree,"* and "can be called *communicable* . . . like receptivity to warmth or infectious [*ansteckender*] diseases . . . since it spreads naturally [*natürlicher Weise*]," and to which there is no obligation. The *Metaphysics of Morals* remarks on sympathy will be discussed in greater detail in the next section.

2.5 Text 5: *Anthropology from a Pragmatic Point of View*, 1798

In *Anthropology from a Pragmatic Point of View* (1798), Kant draws the distinction in the same terms that appear in the *Anthropology Mrongovius* more than a decade earlier: (a) "sensitivity" (*Empfindsamkeit*) and (b) "sentimentality" (*Empfindelei*) (Anth 7:235–6). Kant explains that "Sensitivity . . . is a faculty and a power which either permits or prevents both the state of pleasure as well as displeasure from entering the mind, and thus it possesses choice" (Anth 7:235–6). Here, he explains the *Mrongovius* idea of choosing for others what they will enjoy in more detail (though apparently with misogyny):

---

[9] Interpretative reconstruction of the last sentence in this passage above is required to extract the distinction between moral and instinctive *Sympathie*. The key clause in that sentence is: *"wir würden daher ohne Gedanken keine . . . moralischen Gefühle haben; der Andere würde kein moralisches, sondern nur instinctmäßiges Mitgefühl (Sympathie) äußern können."* Mitgefühl is literally "with-feeling," and the Cambridge edition translates it as "fellow feeling" in this passage, though in passages in other texts, as "shared feeling" (MM 6:443) and "sympathy" (6:320n). The adjacency of *instinctmäßiges Mitgefühl* and *Sympathie* makes it clear that Kant is saying that *instinctmäßiges Mitgefühl* is a kind of *Sympathie*. But the hanging *"moralisches"* must be connected to something later in the sentence, either just *"Mitgefühl,"* or just *"Sympathie,"* or both *"Mitgefühl"* and *"Sympathie."* The natural reading of *"Mitgefühl (Sympathie)"* is that Kant is offering *Sympathie* as a paraphrase of *Mitgefühl*, so it is natural to read *"moralisches"* as connected to both.

"Sensitivity is manly; for the man who wants to spare his wife or children difficulties or pain must possess such fine feeling[t] [*feines Gefühl*] as is necessary in order to judge their sensation not by his own strength but rather by their weakness" (7:236). The connection between *Empfindsamkeit*/*Empfindelei* and sympathy is made explicit when Kant says that *Empfindelei* "is a weakness by which we can be affected, even against our will, by sympathy [*Theilnehmung*] for others' condition who, so to speak, can play at will on the organ of the sentimentalist" (7:236).

2.6 Aggregating Descriptions in the Five Texts

Though these discussions use some different terminology, they all clearly present mutually consistent distinctions between two ways of sympathizing. There are conceptual connections where terminological connections are absent. This makes it reasonable to assume that it is the same distinction in the five passages. We can therefore gather together the descriptions in the five passages to provide a detailed description of the two ways of sympathizing.

The first (a) is rational (Anth-F 25:610; MM 6:456–7). It involves the communication of ideas, concepts, thoughts, and feelings which allow us to sympathize correctly (Anth-F 25:607; Anth-Mr 25:1320; Eth-V 27:677). It is a strength and power which permits us to choose whether others' feelings enter our minds (Anth-Mr 25:1320–1; Anth 7:235–6). It is free and regulated by practical reason, and we are obligated to sympathize in this way (MM 6:456–7).

The second (b) spreads naturally like an infection (MM 6:456–7). It is nonrational or even irrational, and not based on deliberation, and does not afford us the same possibility of sympathizing correctly as rational sympathy (MM 6:456–7; Anth-Mr 25:1320–1; Eth-V 27:677). It is not free in the same way as rational sympathy, and we are not obligated to sympathize in this way: It is a weakness through which others' feelings can enter our minds against our will which is associated with instinct and animality, and it can be driven by affect (MM 6:456–7; Anth 7:236; Eth-V 27:677; Anth-F 25:607–11). We should not read Kant as claiming that natural sympathy is strictly involuntary: If we have the power to choose whether others' feelings enter our minds, then we can exert this power to avoid natural sympathy and instead sympathize rationally. But if we fall into it naturally, then it takes effort and discipline to avoid it. Marcia Baron's term "self-inflicted passivity" (1995: 216) is helpful for describing this kind of involuntariness, and so I will typically describe the contrast between rational and natural sympathy as a contrast between activity and passivity. We should also not read Kant as claiming that natural sympathy is strictly unethical. If rational sympathy is simply natural sympathy harnessed by practical reason, as I will argue, then the capacity for rational sympathy depends on the capacity for natural sympathy. Furthermore, natural sympathy can contingently align our feelings with others' feelings and allow us to naturally adopt their permissible ends as our own.

2.7 Why Does the Distinction Seem Absent in the *Groundwork* and Second *Critique*?

If Kant is committed to a distinction between rational and natural sympathy, and even lectured about it in the same year the *Groundwork* was published, why does he elide or obscure the distinction in the *Groundwork* and the second *Critique*? Marcia Baron suggests that Kant may have felt compelled to "distance himself" from "his earlier endorsement of a version of moral sense theory" in his precritical ethics, in a way that led him to "hyperbole" in his early critical ethics (1995: 204).[10] However, the *Groundwork* and second *Critique* may allow an interpretation according to which they *do* reference this distinction, though obscurely and indirectly.

Kant's most detailed explanations of concepts he uses to characterize the attitude of the *Groundwork* philanthropist, "cold [*kalt*] and indifferent [*gleichgültig*]," (G 4:398), suggest that they stand on the rational side of the distinction between rational and natural sympathy. Lara Denis points out that Kant distinguishes "cold-bloodedness [*Kaltblütigkeit*]" and "*frigidity* [*Kaltsinnigkeit*]" in the Collins Ethics lecture notes. Frigidity is a "want of love" and a "lack of the feeling whereby the state of others affects us," while "cold-bloodedness [*Kaltblütigkeit*] is a want of affect [*Affekts*] in love": "Cold-bloodedness of love^t provides regularity and order" (Kant Eth-C 27:420, Denis 2000: 53). Perhaps this lets us read the cold, indifferent philanthropist as someone whose natural sympathy is extinguished by grief, but who does not become frigid: instead, he sympathizes rationally, by drawing on an active capacity to sympathize in an ordered way. Perhaps this is how he "tears himself out of [the] deadly insensibility" brought on by his grief (G 4:398).[11]

In the *Critique of Practical Reason*, Kant's remarks about sympathy focus on *pathological* sympathy (CPrR 5:85). Pathological feelings are "produced by ... object[s] of the senses" and are distinguished from practical feelings, which are "possible through a preceding (objective) determination of the will and causality of reason" (5:80). Pathological sympathy is thus on the natural side of rational/natural sympathy distinction discussed above. While no remarks in

---

[10] Baron does not argue that Kant has a theory of rational sympathy, but she explores the tensions between Kant's early and late critical ethics in illuminating detail.

[11] Denis (2000) notes the appearance of these terms in the *Groundwork* but does not interpret the *Groundwork* philanthropist in light of the detailed explanations. The detailed explanations arguably offer support for Wood's reading of the *Groundwork* philanthropist (see note 5 above).

the second *Critique* explicitly indicate that sympathy can be a practical feeling, and many remarks indicate that respect is the *only* practical feeling, he draws a suggestive distinction between sympathy which follows and precedes consideration of duty:

> Even [the] feeling [of] tender sympathy, if it precedes consideration of what is duty and becomes the determining ground, is itself burdensome to right-thinking persons, [and] brings their considered maxims into confusion (CPrR 5:118)

Since this passage does not state that sympathy which follows consideration of duty can be rationally willed to follow, this passage does not draw the distinction described in this Element, but perhaps it gestures towards it.

I do not wish to claim that these suggestions for reading the *Groundwork* and the second *Critique* align comfortably with the entirety of these texts. However, they offer, at the very least, points of conceptual connection where Kant could have attached his theory of rational sympathy had he chosen to.

3 A Debate about Translating *Doctrine of Virtue* §§34–5, and a Concern about Passivity

The most important published evidence for the distinction between rational and natural sympathy is in the *Metaphysics of Morals* passages quoted above, which appear in *Doctrine of Virtue* §§34–5, entitled "Sympathetic Feeling Is Generally a Duty" in Mary Gregor's translation (MM 6:456–8). I have adopted Gregor's translation nearly in full. Rudolf Makkreel and Melissa Seymour Fahmy criticize Gregor's translation because they think she unwarrantedly represents *humanitas practica* as a kind of sympathy. They think *humanitas practica* should not be represented as a kind of sympathy because Kant clearly holds that *humanitas practica* is something we can freely will, while Kant seems to think of sympathy as an aspect of love, and claims that we cannot will ourselves to love: "*Love* is a matter of *feeling,* not of willing, and I cannot love because I *will* to" (MM 6:401; Fahmy 2010: 313; Makkreel 2012: 114; also see CPrR 5:83). This makes it seem that sympathy must be passive. First I will explain their challenges to Gregor's translation, and then I will address the concern about passivity.

Rudolf Makkreel argues that the term in the section title which Gregor translates as "sympathetic feeling," *theilnehmende Empfindung,* can be translated as "participatory feeling" (111). He argues that this alternative is preferable, because to begin the section with the claim that "Sympathetic Feeling is Generally a Duty," as Gregor does, is to claim we have a duty to experience feelings that sound too much like *humanitas aesthetica,* which Kant goes on the claim we do *not* have a duty to experience, thereby making a muddle of a pivotal discussion. Makkreel interprets sympathy as an inherently passive feeling, and *theilnehmende Empfindung* as a fundamentally different feeling which is "a more active counterpart to sympathy" and is "not passively received, but a spontaneous expression of 'practical humanity'" (Makkreel 2012: 111).

There is, however, strong support for Gregor's translation in a passage in the Friedländer Anthropology lecture notes:

> Finally ... we can consider sympathetic feeling [*sympathetische Gefühl*]. [The term] sympathy [*Sympathie*] must not be rendered [*übersetzt*] by "compassion" [*Mitleid*], but by "sympathizing" [*Theilnehmung*]. Compassion [*Mitleid*] is more concerned with misfortune. However, we have sympathy [*Sympathie*] also in good fortune. We have compassion [*Mitleid*] for those who are weak, but we have sympathy [*Sympathie*] also with those who are strong. Sympathy [*Sympathie*] is thus the genus and compassion [*Mitleid*] the species. (Anth-F 25:606)

The key word *übersetzt* can also be translated as "translated," and is translated this way elsewhere in the Cambridge translation (CPrR 5:60; MM 6:237). Thus, this passage amounts to Kant's own translation advice on this controversy: He tells us to translate *Sympathie* as *Theilnehmung*. This provides strong evidence that Kant sees no difference between the feelings to which these terms refer.

Melissa Seymour Fahmy offers a different critique of Gregor's translation and addresses the concern about passivity differently. Fahmy highlights Kant's original German description of *humanitas practica*:

> Diese [humanitas] kann nun in dem Vermogen und Willen, sich einander in Ansehung seiner Gefühle mitzuteilen (humanitas practica) ... gesetzt werden. (MM 6:456; Fahmy 2009: 35)

Fahmy argues that to accurately translate this, we should not give Gregor's version, "humanity can be located ... in the *capacity* and the *will* to *share in others' feelings*," but instead "This [humanity] can be located in the capacity and will to communicate with each other in view of (with respect to) one's feelings." She concludes that the duty of *humanitas practica* is not a duty to *have* or *share* feelings, but rather to *communicate about* whatever sympathetic feelings we have (Fahmy 2009: 35). She acknowledges Kant's reference to a duty to "cultivate the compassionate natural ... feelings in us" (MM 6:457), but interprets this as a duty to *strive* to have these feelings, which we can fulfill even if we do not succeed (Fahmy 2010: 321–322, 2019: 418–419).

Fahmy's interpretation is textually well-grounded if we focus just on MM §§34–5. But we often talk of communication and feeling without the prepositional mediation of expressions like *in Ansehung* (with respect to). Communicating feelings can mean that one person conveys feelings to another in such a way that the other experiences the feelings too. In *Doctrine of Virtue*

§34, Kant is clearly using this unmediated sense of "communication" in characterizing *humanitas aesthetica* (what I call the natural side of the distinction) – he says it "can be called *communicable* [*mittheilend*] . . . like receptivity to warmth." The presence of *in Ansehung* in the description of *humanitas practica* does not entail that Kant means to rule *in* communication *about* feelings but rule *out* communication *of* feelings: He may think that *humanitas practica* involves communication *about* feelings which prompts communication *of* feelings.

Evidence that this is indeed what he thinks is provided by the Vigilantius Ethics passage from just a few years before the *Metaphysics of Morals* (1793–4) quoted above, which distinguishes "moral" and "instinctual" sympathy. Let us consider it again at greater length:

> [Friends] stand together, to communicate not only their feelings and sensations to one another, but also their thoughts [*sich nicht allein ihre Gefühle und Empfindungen, sondern auch ihre Gedanken einander mitzuteilen*]. Of these two kinds of communication, the mutual disclosure of thoughts is the best, and is truly the ground for the communication of feeling [*Communication der Gefühle*]. For feelings can be disclosed no otherwise, than by the imparting of thoughts; thus we must have an idea of the feeling in advance, and must hence have employed reason, in order to have known it accurately before we communicate ^{t} it [*ehe wir sie mitteilen*], so that the feeling thereafter may be correct and not instinctual; without thoughts, therefore, we would have no feelings, at least none of a moral kind; the other would be able to express^t [*äußern*] not moral, but only instinctual fellow-feeling (sympathy) [*der Andere würde kein moralisches, sondern nur instinctmäßiges Mitgefühl (Sympathie) äußern können*]. (Eth-V 27:677–8)

In this passage, we have three references to the communication of feeling without any prepositional mediation like *in Ansehung*, all of which are clearly meant to characterize the moral side of the distinction. While Kant also emphasizes the communication of thoughts in this passage, it is clear that the purpose of communicating thoughts is to accurately convey feelings, so that the other can have the feelings too, and by virtue of having them, express moral sympathy. Thus, here too, we see that Kant's lecture notes provide support for Gregor's translation, and so we should think that he really is telling us that sympathetic feeling is generally a duty, and that fulfilling it involves the will and capacity to share others' feelings (MM 6:456).

Embracing the idea that morality requires us to have sympathetic feelings, as the account presented here does, poses its own interpretative challenge. In what sense can we actively or spontaneously prompt sympathetic feelings in ourselves? Kant clearly thinks there is something important in the point that we cannot will ourselves to love (MM 6:401, quoted above). The thought that "we have no direct control over our feelings," as Korsgaard puts it (1996: 182), seems accurate not only to Kant's ethics but also to the everyday phenomenology of feeling. However, Kant also holds that we can come to love people through the *practice of acting* beneficently: "*Beneficence* is a duty. If someone practices [*ausübt*] it often ... he eventually comes actually to love the person he has helped" (MM 6:402). According to the Collins Ethics notes, "if I love others from obligation ... by practice [*Uebung*] it becomes love from inclination" (Eth-C 27:419). Thus, Kant's more nuanced view appears to be that we *can* control feelings of love in an important sense, because we can freely adopt practices that prompt such feelings. Kant's account of rational sympathy also includes the notions of action and practice. As discussed in more detail below, rational sympathy is a skill in performing *mental* actions which prompt feelings, and Kant says it is a *skill that we can acquire by practice*:

> [T]he power to transpose the I is necessary, and to put oneself in the point of view and place of the other, so that one thinks with him, and has sympathy with him ᵗ [*sich in ihm fühlt*]. ... To take a point of view is a skill [*Geschicklichkeit*] which one can acquire by practice [*sich durch Uebung erwerben kann*]. (Anth-F 25:475)

If we *can* acquire a skill, then it is deontically consistent for reason to tell us that we *ought* to acquire it, and if we can acquire it by *practice*, reason can tell us that we ought to practice until we acquire it. When we have acquired a skill, we have volitional control over the skill. This passage implies that rational sympathy is such a skill, and that when we have acquired it, we can mentally act in ways that prompt sympathetic feeling. As discussed in greater detail below, the "power to transpose the I" (ibid.) is a skill of imagination, and the locus of volitional control in rational sympathy is in imagining, not in feeling. Natural and rational sympathy can involve qualitatively identical sympathetic joys and pains but are differently oriented to practical reason. The actions in rational sympathy involve imaginatively adopting another's subjective viewpoint on the world, and imagining intuitional content to furnish that viewpoint. We acquire the sympathetic feelings themselves *in response* to these reason-guided imaginings, *not* by willing the feelings to spontaneously spring forth. In this way, rational sympathy fits the description of moral feeling in *Theory and Practice*: It is "not the cause but the effect of the determination of the will" (TP 8:283).

4 Sympathy and the Imagination

Kant describes sympathy as a function of the imagination in multiple passages. He says that sympathy is "an effect of imagination" (MM 6:321 n; also see

6:457), and he refers to the "sympathetic power of imagination" (Anth 7:179; also see 7:238). If sympathy is a function of imagination, then the difference between rational and natural sympathy must be a difference between two ways the imagination can function: an active, reason-guided way and a passive way.

Imagination is a fundamental power in Kant's theory of mind, one of two "parts" of sensibility, the other of which is "sense" (Anth 7:153). Sense is the "faculty of intuition in the presence of an object," while imagination is "intuition even without the presence of an object" (ibid.; also see B151). A key function of imagination is to make connections that are different from the logical relations between concepts, but which are nonetheless necessary for experience.

In the first *Critique*'s Transcendental Deduction, an aspect of imagination that Kant calls a priori productive imagination plays a role in spontaneously structuring sensibility as a part of the transcendental synthesis, which makes a priori cognition possible (see e.g. B151-2; Anth 7:167, 174). In this role, the imagination is responsible for what Kant calls the *figurative synthesis* of the manifold of sensible intuition (B151-4), one aspect of which is the establishment of a priori connections among times to form the schemata necessary for the application of a priori concepts of the understanding, that is, the categories of the understanding (A142-5/B182-5).

The imagination plays a crucial role a posteriori as well. It provides schemata for empirical rather than a priori concepts (B179-81/A140-2) and contributes to the generation of empirical concepts. Its activities make up much of the mental contents of our waking and dreaming lives. Passively received sensible content is due to sense, and transitions between mental states are the work of the understanding or reason insofar as they are guided by active reasoning, but Kant thinks that the rest of the contents of intuition and transitions between mental states are the work of the imagination.

Even when reasoning is involved in the functioning of the imagination, Kant seems to think that the role of reasoning is merely to direct the imagination. The Friedländer Anthropology says "[t]he power of choice can only do something insofar as it gives direction to the imagination and then it straightaway runs according to its new direction, like water in the stream" (Anth-F 25:515), and that when the imagination is not "subjugated to the power of choice" it is "often the path of many vices" (ibid.). The Mrongovius Anthropology says that if we do not choose the direction of the imagination, "[t]he imagination directs itself according to the inclinations" – for example, "[i]f one feels hatred, then the imagination shows everything from its most detestable side" (Anth-Mr 25:1260). The Collins Ethics calls our power to choose the direction of the imagination a "monarchy":

> The power that the soul has over all its faculties ... to subordinate them to its free choice, without being necessitated to do so, is a monarchy. If man does not busy himself with this monarchy, he is a plaything of other forces and impressions, against his choice ... If he does not have himself under control, his imagination has free play; he cannot discipline himself, but is carried away by it[.] (Eth-C 27:362)[12]

These ideas, along with the points about the hazards of affect in natural sympathy which we saw above, make it reasonable to think of natural sympathy as an aspect of the incessant passive churn of the imagination. The idea that it is constantly at work in us, even when it is not actively regulated by reason, helps explain Kant's thought above that natural sympathy is "like receptivity to warmth or contagious diseases" (MM 6:409). Assuming that we are not telepaths, feeling cannot be directly conveyed from the minds of others; however, if sympathy is part of the constant passive roving of our imaginations, it makes sense to think it would have a phenomenology such that sympathetic feelings seep into our sensibility unbidden, like sensations of temperature or disease symptoms.[13] This suggests that we can in turn understand rational sympathy as the voluntary guiding of the imaginative associations we make while sympathizing, so that we sympathize correctly (accurately and morally).

Kant distinguishes between two kinds of productive imagination: an "a priori" and "a posteriori" kind. The first *Critique*'s discussion of productive imagination emphasizes a priori productive imagination, which (as mentioned above) is responsible for the transcendental figurative synthesis of the sensible manifold (B151-4), and its discussion of a posteriori imagination emphasizes a posteriori reproductive imagination. But a posteriori imagination has both reproductive and productive faculties, and both are important in understanding sympathy. Reproductive imagination, which is exclusively a posteriori, "brings back to the mind an empirical intuition that it had previously" (Anth 7:167; also see B152, Anth-F 25:512, and Anth-Mr 25:1257). A posteriori productive imagination possesses a kind of spontaneity which reproductive imagination lacks, and which is different from the kind of spontaneity possessed by a priori productive imagination. Kant says a posteriori imagination is "*inventive*," though "not exactly *creative*" (Anth 7:168). While it does not merely bring previous empirical intuition back to the mind in the way reproductive imagination does, "it is not capable of producing a sense representation that was *never* given to our faculty of sense. One can always furnish evidence of the material of

---

[12] The power of monarchy appears to be closely related to what Kant calls "autocracy" in the *Metaphysics of Morals* (6:383). See Baxley (2010) for a helpful discussion.

[13] See Timmermann (2016) for a helpful discussion of this aspect of natural sympathy.

its ideas" (Anth 7:168). It is nonetheless "very powerful in creating, as it were, another nature, out of the material which the real one gives it" (CPJ 5:314).

The fact that a posteriori productive imagination must draw on representations previously given to sense may suggest that its spontaneity is of a lower order than the spontaneity of a priori productive imagination, since the latter involves determining the spatiality and temporality of things in sensibility which in themselves have no temporality or spatiality. In this sense, it arguably makes a more fundamentally novel contribution to human experience than a posteriori productive imagination. On the other hand, there is no scope in the activity of the a priori productive imagination for the spontaneity of transcendentally free *moral* action, and the a posteriori productive imagination has this kind of spontaneity when guided by practical reason, as it is in rational sympathy. To keep things concise, "productive imagination" is used henceforth just to refer to a posteriori productive imagination.

Kant's description of the distinction between reproductive and productive imagination makes it intuitive to think that sympathy involves the productive imagination. Representing some of our feelings as *shared* or *like another's* requires us to represent them as something more than mere recapitulations of our own experiences. However, if we assume we are not telepaths, then we can only aim at having feelings like another's by drawing on our own previous experiences in creative ways. But as we will shortly see in more detail, sympathy requires the functions of reproductive imagination too.

Productive imagination can function both actively and passively. Kant often describes this as a distinction between voluntariness and involuntariness (Anth 7:174; Anth-Mr 25:1257). However, as mentioned earlier, the fact that we can regulate the imagination implies that the passive functioning of the imagination cannot be strictly involuntary. It is instead a self-inflicted passivity. Passive productive imagination is called "fantasy" (*Phantasie*) (Anth 7:167, 7:175; also see Anth-Mr 25:1258, Met-Mr 29:884–5). Kant makes an explicit connection between fantasy and sympathy in the third *Critique*:

> [T]he **emotions** that can reach the strength of an affect are also quite diverse. We have **brave** as well as **tender** emotions. The latter, if they reach the level of an affect, are good for nothing at all; the tendency toward them is called **oversensitivity** [*Empfindelei*]. A sympathetic pain [*theilnehmender Schmerz*] that will not let itself be consoled, or with which, when it concerns invented evils, we consciously become involved, to the point of being taken in by the fantasy [*Phantasie*], as if it were real, proves and constitutes a tenderhearted but at the same time weak soul, which reveals a beautiful side, and which can certainly be called fantastic [*phantastisch*] ... (CPJ 5:273)

The term translated here as "oversensitivity" (*Empfindelei*) is the same as the term we saw translated as "sentimentality" in Section 2. Since the sympathy of *Empfindelei* is natural sympathy, the connection Kant makes at CPJ 5:273 between *Empfindelei*, *Theilnehmung*, and *Phantasie* implies that natural sympathy is a species of fantasy and is thus a species of passive productive imagination.

We can maintain the symmetry in the distinction between rational and natural sympathy in the texts considered thus far if we suppose that rational sympathy is a species of the rational counterpart to fantasy, which Kant calls "disciplined fantasy <*phantasia subacta*>" (Met-Mr 29:885).[14] This makes rational sympathy a species of active productive imagination. It is worth noting that Kant appears to use "disciplined fantasy" as equivalent to terms he uses for the productive imagination of artists – that is, "fabrication" ("*Erfindung*," Anth 7:175; "*Erdichtung*," Met-Mr 29:885) and "composition [*Composition*]" (Anth 7:175). This might seem to suggest that we are on the wrong track, since the kind of imagination involved in rational sympathy and creating art might strike some as quite different. However, as we will see in more detail later, Kant thinks that art and sympathy involve the imagination in similar ways.

Productive imagination must also draw on the powers of reproductive imagination. Reproductive imagination is entirely governed by what Kant calls the "law" (or sometimes "laws") of "association," but the productive imagination is not (CPJ 5:240, 269, 314; Anth-F 25:512; and Anth-Mr 25:1272). The law of association is that "empirical ideas that have frequently followed one another produce a habit in the mind such that when one idea is produced, the other also comes into being" (Anth 7:176). Through this law, "ideas that were often connected with present ones ... are produced" (Anth-Mr 25:1273). The point that the productive imagination can organize itself according to this law is implicitly established by the fact that Kant states the law of association in the *Anthropology* in a section entitled "On sensibility's productive faculty of association" (Anth 7:176).

Let us approach the question of how the law of association functions in productive imagination by first considering how it functions in reproductive imagination. In reproductive imagination, the law of association determines which previous intuitions are recapitulated in response to one's current sense contents:

> For example, if we see smoke, then the representation of fire immediately appears. If the clock strikes at whichever time one is accustomed to eat, and one hears it striking, then the representation of food immediately appears. (Anth-F 25:512)

---

[14] The translators note that "in his *Metaphysica*, §571, Baumgarten translates *phantasia subacta* as *wohlgeordnete Einbildungskraft* (well-ordered power of imagination)" (Kant 1997b: 253).

These habitual associations are the empirical-psychological foundation of our capacities to inductively generate new beliefs about empirical laws.[15] But reproductive imagination and its law of association are not limited to temporal order. Kant says it also associates intuitions based on "contiguity," which he also calls "unity of place" (Anth-F 25:513), and this creates the subjective unity of space which, along with the subjective unity of time, subjectively unifies the empirical form of intuition. Last but not least, it associates intuition based on "similarity," which he also calls "affinity" (Anth-F 25:513; A766/B794), and this kind of association underwrites our empirical-psychological capacity to generate empirical concepts, as well as our ability to call up imagined intuitional content to accompany concepts.

The associations made by the reproductive imagination produce subjective "unity of given representations" which we then incorporate into "objective unity" by testing them with judgments according to the categories of the understanding, to ensure that "representations are combined in the object ... regardless of any difference in the condition of the subject" (B141-2). The subjective unity produced by the reproductive imagination and the objective unity synthesized according to the categories differs in that the subjective unity is unified from the *first-person standpoint* of the particular human subject who does the unifying, while the objective unity is one which would be cognized by *any human subject* who synthesizes experience according to the categories.

As noted above, the productive imagination is not entirely governed by the law of association in the way the reproductive imagination is – this is what makes it productive rather than merely reproductive. The productive imagination's freedom from the law of association is both hazardous and valuable. It is hazardous because it can lead not only to inadequately disciplined fantasy which prompts affect, as it does in natural sympathy, but also to a "ruleless fantasy" which "approaches madness, where fantasy plays completely with the human being and the unfortunate victim has no control at all over the course of his representations" – its inventions cannot "find their place in a possible world," "because they are self-contradictory" (Anth 7:181). It is valuable because freedom from the law of association also allows disciplined fantasy, of which art and rational sympathy are species. In disciplined fantasy, the imagination cannot be entirely governed by the law of association, but it must regulate itself according to laws in *some* sense if its productions are to be

---

[15] Kant famously claims that Hume goes wrong in thinking that these associations generate our concept of cause as well – he thinks Hume fails to realize that the possibility of temporal order itself depends upon a transcendentally prior pure synthesis of imagination (A 766–7/B794-5; P 4:257–8).

possible in imaginary worlds. On this point, let us consider at greater length a passage quoted earlier:

> The imagination (as a productive cognitive faculty) is ... very powerful in creating, as it were, another nature, out of the material which the real one gives it. ... [W]e transform the latter, no doubt always in accordance with analogous laws, but also in accordance with principles that lie higher in reason (and which are every bit as natural to us as those in accordance with which the understanding apprehends empirical nature); in this we feel our freedom from the law of association ... in accordance with which material can certainly be lent to us by nature, but the latter can be transformed by us into something entirely different. (CPJ 5:314)

When Kant says productive imagination allows us to "transform the material which the real" nature gives us according to "analogous laws," it is not clear whether the analogous laws he has in mind are analogous laws of nature, or of association – he refers to nature (though not natural laws) in the previous sentence, and he refers to "the law of association" later in the same sentence. It is plausible that both play roles in productive imagination's transformation of material from real nature into another nature.

The context for this passage is a discussion of art. It makes sense to think disciplined fantasy would sometimes produce fictional worlds with natural laws different from, but analogous to, our own, though presumably not too different: Fairy tales are salient examples, and Kant objects to them because they strain children's imaginations, so he seems to regard them as examples of insufficiently disciplined fantasy (Ped 9:476; also see OFBS 2:214). Fictional worlds typically differ most from the actual world in the invention of fictional initiating events, from which the plot proceeds according to laws not discernibly different from the actual laws. However, when we draw on disciplined fantasy for the purpose of sympathizing with actual people, we are presumably required to imagine their lives as governed by the laws of the actual world, so while the notion of analogous natural laws is useful in thinking about fiction, it seems to add no useful detail to our picture of rational sympathy.

It is plausible to think that a disciplined fictional world must also provide, through the perspective of a character within it, an imagined subjective unity like that which the reproductive imagination creates when it follows the law of association. Just as we can build a fictional world by creatively imagining fictional events from which the story proceeds according to laws much like those of our own world, we can build a fictional world by imaginatively stepping into the first-person standpoint of a fictional character, and making associations according to principles of association much like those we apply from our own first-person perspectives, as we empirically synthesize our own subjective unities. This activity of productive imagination makes sense to posit not only in relation to fictional characters but also in relation to actual people with whom we sympathize.

5 Putting Ourselves in Others' Places

Kant says that the sympathetic imagination puts us "in the other's place" (Anth-F 25:575; for similar language, see MM 6:321 n; Eth-H 27:58, 65; and Anth-F 25:607).[16] Kant does not describe this process in as much detail as one might wish, but the basic idea is clear: We take up the other's first-person standpoint in imagination. It is noteworthy that the line between *really* occupying a first-person standpoint and *imagining* doing so is in a sense thinner with respect to Kant's theory of imagination than it is with respect to the everyday notion of imagination. That is, according to Kant's account of experience, I put myself in my *own* place through an activity of the a posteriori imagination, which involves empirically unifying passively received sensible content with reproduced sensible content, and thereby empirically synthesizing a subjectively unified viewpoint on the world. Kant does not explicitly characterize putting ourselves in others' places in terms of the imagination's work of subjective synthesis, but it is plausible to suppose that he has such an account in mind. The reproductive imagination is what provides the subjective unity which puts me in my own place, so it is reasonable to suppose that it is the reproductive imagination's capacities placed in the harness of productive imagination which allow me to put myself in another's place. Kant claims that it is this imaginative activity which creates sympathy, and which finds its most complete form in the ideal of friendship, an "ideal of each sympathizing with and communicating about the other's wellbeing ᵗ [*Ideal der Theilnehmung und Mittheilung an dem Wohl eines jeden*]" (MM 6:469; also see Eth-V 27:677–8, quoted above) which guides us to strive toward a "maximum" (MM 6:469) of sympathy in which "each mutually shares in every situation of the other, as if it were encountered by himself" (Eth-V 27:677).

Putting ourselves in others' places is necessary but not sufficient for prompting sympathetic feelings. We can put ourselves into a universal position: When following the second "maxim of the common human understanding," one "think[s] in the position of everyone else" to reflect on his "own judgement from a universal standpoint ... which he can only determine by putting himself into the standpoint of others" (CPJ 5:294–5; also see Anth 7:228). We can also "put ourselves in the position of another" in a merely "logical [*logisch*],"

---

[16] Makkreel (2012: 109) and Timmermann (n.d.) discuss imaginative projection and sympathy, but do not connect this to subjective synthesis or the third *Critique* ideas discussed below.

"heuristic [*hevristisch*]" way, for example "a follower of Crusius," to "get better at certain things" (Eth-H 27:58), such as understanding the structure of another's philosophical views. Neither of these necessarily prompts sympathy. But when we put ourselves in another's place for the purpose of sympathetic participation, this yields "true *sympathy* [*wahrhaftigen Sympathie*], where we really feel [*fühlen*] ourselves to be in his place" (Eth-H 27:58), and "[w]e are sensible of this sympathizing feeling in our entire soul" (Anth-F 25:606). In natural sympathy, we find ourselves imaginatively adopting others' perspectives passively, but adopting others' perspectives is a "skill which one can acquire by practice" (Anth-F 25:475, quoted above), and when we have acquired it, we can do it actively in rational sympathy.

In what may be Kant's most detailed remark on the phenomenon, he says that it occurs with reference to both fictional and actual (historical) people:

> When we read something, a history or a novel, we always put ourselves in the other's place and this is sympathy[t] [*Theilnehmung*]. Every human being as person or as intelligence, relates all thoughts to himself by means of the I; there is nothing in the whole world closer to him than himself. Thus in his own regard he is a focal point of the world, but if he relates everything exclusively to himself, then he makes himself the center. Every human being is a focal point of the world, but not the center. (Anth-F 25:476)

The contrast Kant makes here between the world's foci and its center is expressed in precritical terminology, but it is recognizable as a progenitor of the contrast between subjective and objective unities of experience.

Two passages about sympathy and social subordination in the Friedländer Anthropology provide helpful detail about how voluntarily putting ourselves in others' places molds our sympathetic feelings. One passage is about expanding the range of our feelings to sympathize more correctly with how the other feels. Kant says that "a humble person can easily put himself in the position of the higher one and assume greater dispositions. However, the distinguished one cannot assume the state of the humble one, hence he also does not sympathize [*sympathesirt*] with his misfortune" (Anth-F 25:607). "If the ills are natural, for example, famine, then the distinguished person sympathizes with the humble one just as well as the latter with him, but in the case of ... ideal ills, the distinguished one does not sympathize [*sympathesirt*] with the humble one, but the latter does in fact sympathize [*sympathesirt*] with the former" (25:606–7). The distinguished one "thinks that the one who is thus not accustomed to the refined life is indeed just a humble man, hence he always gets on [in life], if he can just live," and does "not become as aware" of the "distance" of the humble man's "social standing from the civic one in general" (25:607). Kant says that while a commoner "has compassion [*Mitleiden*] for an unfortunate king," the "unfortunate thing with kings" is that they "have no inclination" to "imagine the misfortune of their subjects" (ibid.).

As we saw earlier, when the imagination roves passively, it is guided by inclination, and (ironically, given the passage currently under consideration) we must exercise the power of "monarchy" to actively direct it (Anth-Mr 25:1260; Eth-C 27:362). Kant's implicit point in the passage about class and sympathy is that when the "distinguished" sympathize naturally, their inclinations may dispose them to imagine what it is like for the "humble" to be hungry or in pain, but not to imagine their "ideal" misfortunes. They do not imagine that the "humble" could have ideas about life that include more than just living, which their social standing prevents them from actualizing. The "distinguished" should resist their inclinations, and sympathize correctly, in a way that brings them a greater range of sympathetic feelings.[17]

A second passage on this theme appears nearby, where Kant argues that

> [I]f people ... subordinate to the aristocracy ... are constantly under oppression, then they lose the idea of the right of humanity, for since they have no examples where justice prevails, then they think it must be so. There we must sympathize [*sympathesiren*] with the other's right, but not with the physical ill ... (Anth-F 25:606)

The frequency with which the oppressed lose the idea of right is certainly debatable, and we must be cautious about cultural bias in assuming that social structures which people do not actually resent are really oppressive. But if it is clear that a society is oppressive, then we should sympathize with people who manage to live under that oppression without occurrent resentment by projecting ourselves into a version of their position inflected by the idea of right. Thus, while our primary task in rational sympathy is to be accurate to others' actual feelings, we should in some cases sympathize with the feelings they would have if they experienced their oppression emotionally, by adjusting our sympathies in light of ideas of reason. In this way, we can access feelings on their behalf, which we may be able to help them experience if we can do so without paternalism.

---

[17] Kant sometimes says sympathetic feeling can serve as a support system that can make up for deficits in practical reasoning. For example, at AP 7:253, Kant describes compassion [*Mitleids*] as a "temporary surrogate of reason" which can "handle the reins *provisionally*, until reason has achieved the necessary strength." How can it be true that sympathetic feeling can be prompted by reason, but also serve as a surrogate for it? When we are fortunate, natural sympathy contingently causes us to conform to duty. This is a hazardous contingency, as natural sympathy is vulnerable not only to affect, but also to bias. Kant is especially attuned to classism, as demonstrated by the passage just discussed, but biases like racism, sexism, nationalism, and gender and religious bigotry also deform natural sympathy. Rational sympathy corrects for such biases.

The discussions in this section and the previous section, concerning productive imagination, subjective synthesis, and putting ourselves in others' places, have outlined a theory of what we might call the *form* of rational sympathy. That is, we empirically knit together intuitional contents we imagine the other to have by associating them in terms of their imagined space, time, and similarity relations, thereby allowing us to occupy an imaginary first-person perspective for the other. But we do not yet have a theory of the *content* of rational sympathy. How do we produce the imagined intuitional content which we are meant to have under active control in rational sympathy, such as the additional imagined content that the kings discussed above ought to have? Kant's answer, briefly sketched in Section 2, has to do with communicating our feelings so that others can sympathize correctly (Eth-V 27:677). As will be discussed in the next section, this requires us to draw on our ability to regulate our imagination by controlling our associations in communicating how we feel and understanding others' communications of their feelings.

6 Correctly Communicating Feeling

We can learn about Kant's theory of how we populate imagined first-person perspectives of others with imagined sensible content by studying the connection noted earlier between sympathy and art. Both sympathy and art require us to communicate feelings, and both involve imaginatively putting ourselves in another person's place, whether it is an actual or fictional person. The third *Critique* outlines a theory of how this communication works.

Kant thinks that sympathy is always a matter of putting ourselves in others' places. The Friedländer passage cited in Section 2 states that we must do this "when we read something" (Anth-F 25:476), which suggests that we must always do this when we read literature. The third *Critique* makes no similarly general claim, but it does state that such imaginative projection is a way to engage art:

> [A] certain poet says in the description of a beautiful morning: "The sun streamed forth, as tranquillity streams from virtue." The consciousness of virtue, when one puts oneself, even if only in thought, in the place of a virtuous person, spreads in the mind a multitude of sublime and calming feelings[.] (CPJ 5:316)

Kant's idea here is that concepts communicated by the poet to the reader prompt the reader to put herself in the place of a character and imagine those concepts applying to her, and that this sparks associations in the reader's imagination which prompt feelings. If we assume that we can use the same powers of the imagination in sympathy that we use in the kind of case Kant mentions in this passage, then further details about how the imagination works in this kind of case are also applicable to the sympathetic imagination.

The "beautiful morning" passage just quoted is one of two examples Kant offers of "aesthetic ideas." Aesthetic ideas are central in his account of communicating feeling through artistic language. Kant says that an aesthetic idea is a "representation of the imagination associated with a given concept" (CPJ 5:316), but in aesthetic ideas, the relationship between representations of the imagination and concepts differs from the relationship that obtains when the imagination relates representations to concepts for purposes of cognition (5:316–7). It is not clear from the text whether aesthetic ideas include feelings, or we respond to aesthetic ideas by having feelings. But it is clear that when one successfully expresses an aesthetic idea by means of expressing the associated concept in language, one is able to prompt another person to have feelings like one's own feelings about the aesthetic idea (5:317). The capacity to form aesthetic ideas is "genius," and the capacity to express them is "spirit" (5:317), and while artists we call geniuses are "exemplary" in their exercise of these capacities (5:318), these capacities are "really only a talent (of the imagination)" (5:314) which we all have in one degree or another. What Kant is describing in the "beautiful morning" passage is the expression of an aesthetic idea by way of concepts, which the recipient receives by imaginatively putting herself in the place of someone to whom those concepts apply, in a way that allows the recipient to have feelings like the feelings the imagined person has.

To explain how this works, Kant contrasts two uses of imagination, one "for cognition" (CPJ 5:316), and another "through which the subjective disposition of the mind ... can be communicated to others" (5:317), including "inner feeling" (5:296), which Kant regards as a subjective aspect of sensible content. We use imagination in the latter way when we communicate aesthetic ideas. When we use the imagination for cognition, "the imagination is under the constraint of the understanding and is subject to the limitation of being adequate to its concept" (5:316–7); concepts and the intuitions provided by imagination "flow together into a cognition" (5:296) as we attend to the aspects of our subjective unity that can be synthesized into the objective unity. The aspect of the imagination which assembles intuitions for synthesis into objectivity is reproductive imagination, as discussed in Section 4.

When we use the imagination for communication of aesthetic ideas, the imagination and understanding are related differently: "The imagination is free to provide, beyond ... concord with the concept," a "manifold of ... representations in the free use of the imagination" which the "imagination ... associates with" that concept. These freely associated representations "belong to the concept" but "aesthetically enlarge ... the concept itself in an unbounded way," and this "arouses a multitude of sensations and supplementary representations" which prompt feelings (CPJ 5:316–7). In the "beautiful morning" passage, the poet's goal is to convey the "multitude of sublime and calming feelings" she has when she thinks about virtue, and she does this by carefully making free associations to select concepts she thinks will prompt the reader to imagine things that will prompt her to have those same sublime and calming feelings. The reader puts herself in the place of the character presented by the poet, understands the concepts as applying to herself, imagines sensory content based on them, and has feelings in response to this content, which are like the feelings the poet seeks to convey.

Given Kant's focus on art here, he is especially interested in simile. He appears to think that it is straightforwardly true of virtue that tranquility streams from it in a way that is like the way sunlight streams forth – this is what he means in saying that this representation "belongs" to the concept. But this representation is not essential for using the concept in all cases – we need not have it in mind to correctly use it, and another person need not have in mind to understand what we mean in saying "virtue." It is instead something that the poet associates with the concept in her own imagination, choosing it with the goal of helping the reader imagine sensory content which prompts the multitude of sublime and calming feelings.

Something similar happens in conversations in which we seek to sympathize. Kant thinks of poems on the same model we saw him use above for novels, that is, as fictions with which we engage by identifying with fictional characters, so he says readers acquire feelings like those of the poet by imaginatively putting themselves in the place of a fictional person the poet presents. In communication aimed at creating or refining sympathy, the only perspectives we need to include in our model are the perspectives of the person communicating about her feelings and the person seeking to sympathize. We do sometimes use similes in such conversations. The "humble" person in the Friedländer Anthropology may say to the "distinguished" person that anxiety over his children's next meal is like being in a fog, or having a weight pressing upon him. However, much of the basic structure Kant describes in his remarks about aesthetic ideas is found in conversations meant to convey feelings which do not involve literary devices. Because a concept is necessarily general and abstract, there are infinite specific, concrete intuitions which "belong" to that concept in the sense of being appropriately subsumable under it, any of which can be coherently associated with it by the imagination, but none of which are essential to the meaning of the concept, in the sense that none of these particular intuitions are such that the imagination must associate them with the concept for the concept to be understood. Concepts are all that we immediately convey when we communicate in language, and so we have the freedom to associate an infinite variety of intuitions with what language conveys to us. This is part of the "free play" of the imagination Kant discusses in the third *Critique* (e.g. CPJ 5:217, 5:238, 5:240, and 5:256). Given the finitude of experienced time and of the number of associations we can actually make, however, the variety of intuitions we associate with the concepts conveyed to us in language is sharply finite, and since different associated intuitions prompt different feelings, it makes a difference to our feelings that we associate some intuitions rather than others.

The passages we saw earlier about the continuous functioning of imagination imply that our imaginations always follow along in any conversation, in at least a passive way, and associate imagined intuitional content with concepts. If natural sympathy is part and parcel of that constant passive churn, then natural sympathy can arise at any time as a by-product of our conversations. This is valuable when it contingently prompts morally useful insights, and it is problematic when it surprises us with affect or disposes us to act wrongly.

We can also actively exercise our capacity to associate intuitional content with concepts. The ability to do this is really just the productive correlate of reproductive imagination's capacity to associate intuitions according to similarity in the use or generation of empirical concepts. In the productive case, it is the ability to inventively (as it were) "backtrack" from a concept to intuitional content that embodies that concept in a way that is effective for the conversation at hand. When we converse in order to sympathize, responding with feeling to the imagined intuitional content associated with the concepts communicated is the point of the conversation. The communicator can freely select the concepts she thinks are most likely to prompt imagined intuitional content in the sympathizer which will in turn prompt feelings like hers. On the other end of the conversation, the sympathizer must exercise discipline to associate imagined intuitional content she thinks likely to help her sympathize correctly. This makes a "lawful business" of the imagination's "free play," to borrow an idea from Kant's discussion of the sublime (CPJ 5:269). If the "humble" person says to the "distinguished" person, "I would like just one day when people like you spoke with me as if my opinions mattered," the "distinguished" person can discipline her imagination to associate remembered sensible content from moments in her own life when her opinions were not respected, and imagine living a life where her opinions were never respected, and thereby prompt more accurate sympathetic feelings. This provides the *content* of rational sympathy which populates the *form* of rational sympathy described in preceding sections.

An important disanalogy between literature and sympathy is that Kant thinks we can know a priori that the feelings of a poet who writes beautiful poems are universally communicable, but we have no such knowledge regarding many of the feelings we seek to communicate through sympathy.[18] Kant thinks that the pleasure we take in beauty is the result of judging that the contents of the imagination, even in its free play, are nonetheless harmonious with the understanding, in a way that makes this "relation suited to cognition in general" (CPJ 5:217–8). It is a pleasure that results from judging that it is possible to bring aspects of our subjective unity to objectivity. Kant thinks that because cognition is universally communicable, pleasure in the possibility of cognition must be universally communicable too. Kant also thinks we know a priori that feelings about sublimity and morality are universally communicable. But Kant thinks we cannot know a priori that the contingent feelings with which we often sympathize can be universally communicated (CPJ 5:213, 224). This does not entail that we do *not* communicate contingent feelings or that we do not *know* we communicate them. We have seen numerous texts that show Kant thinks we often succeed in communicating contingent feelings in sympathy. Presumably, the kinds of cases he addresses provide empirical grounds for *knowing* that they are often communicable. Thus we *do* have knowledge that contingent feelings can often be communicated in sympathy, but it is a posteriori knowledge.[19]

This suggests that we learn whether and to what degree contingent feelings can be communicated *by communicating*, and continuing to communicate, and through this process discovering where our sympathies are incorrect, and endeavoring to correct them through trial and error. If rational sympathy is necessary to fulfill the duty to take others' ends as our own, as will be argued below, then the lack of a priori knowledge and imperfect universality in sympathy need not pose a moral problem. The duty to take others' ends as our own is imperfect, so it can be fulfilled by imperfect sympathizers.

7 What Problem in Kant's Ethics Is Solved by Rational Sympathy?

As discussed in the introduction, "exclusion" and "inclusion" are two strategies for handling the moral role given to sympathy in the *Metaphysics of Morals* which can appear to be ruled out by the *Groundwork* and second *Critique*. Exclusion aims at explaining the larger role for sympathy in the *Metaphysics of Morals* by housing sympathy in parts of moral deliberation and motivation that are external to the activity of autonomous willing. The goal of exclusion is to

---

[18] Wood (2008: 176) and Fahmy (2009: 45) mention the relationship between sympathy and Kant's discussion of shared feeling in the third *Critique,* but do not note this disanalogy.

[19] Alix Cohen notes that Kant claims that even when it comes to our highly contingent tastes in food and drink, a "comparatively universal validity" can be found if "the host makes his decisions with the tastes of his guests in mind, so that everyone can find something to his liking" (Cohen 2008: 316; AP 7:242). Kant makes a similar point at CPJ 5:213, and states that comparative universality is founded on "empirical rules."

show that, even in the *Metaphysics of Morals*, sympathy is *not* strictly speaking *necessary*, and the essential moral motivation is still being performed by respect for law. Inclusion seeks to identify a *rational* way of sympathizing that is *part* of the activity of the autonomous will, so that sympathy can have standing as a genuinely moral motive alongside respect. The exposition thus far has presented a variety of texts that draw a clear distinction between rational and natural sympathy and contribute to a theory of how rational sympathy works. This suggests that the inclusive approach is worth exploring. However we do not yet have an explanation of why sympathy is necessary in moral motivation. The explanation to be provided can be framed as an answer to this question: What is the problem in Kant's rationalist ethics which requires sympathy for its solution? This section argues that the problem is about taking others' ends as one's own, in cases where those ends are valuable only because they are set by rational agents. Prior to explaining the problem, the stage must be set by describing the duty to take others' ends as one's own, and outlining an important thread in Kant's argument for moral rationalism.

The categorical imperative, as expressed in the formula of humanity, is as follows: "*[s]o act that you use humanity, whether in your own person or in the person of any other, always at the same time as an end, never merely as a means*" (G 4:429). This requires us (1) to never use a human being "merely as a means" (G 4:429), and (2) to try to "further the ends of others," since "the ends of a subject who is an end in itself must ... be also my ends" (G 4:430). The latter of these two requirements is the duty of beneficence. Others have ends that are moral (obligatory or meritorious) for them to pursue, and ends that are subjective, that is, ends which they have due to features of their sensibilities that are contingent from the perspective of rational agency. Agents set subjective ends because they think they will make them happy, due to the specific constitution of their feelings of pleasure and pain which gives them their contingent sensibilities. The duty of beneficence clearly extends to others' subjective ends.

Kant also describes the duty of beneficence as the duty of making others' *happiness* one's end (MM 6:452; also see CPrR 5:34). The explanations of the duty of beneficence in terms of subjective ends and happiness fit together: Happiness is itself a subjective end (G 4:396, CPJ 5:437, MM 6:388) which is the "sum" of our other, more particular subjective ends (CPJ 5:531, TP 8:282–3). Thus jointly taking another's subjective ends as one's ends entails taking her happiness as one's end.

There are limits on the obligation to take others' subjective ends as our own. One limit is that we must refuse to take others' *impermissible* ends as our own (MM 6:388, 450). Because of this, and to be clear and concise, I will often label ends that are subjective and permissible as MPEs. Another limit is that, as an imperfect duty, the duty of beneficence "has in it a latitude for doing more or less, and no specific limits can be assigned to what should be done" (MM 6:393). We must take some subjective ends of some others as our own, and it is meritorious to take more such ends of more others as our own. However, as Baron and Fahmy emphasize, "the idea is not to be equally beneficent to everyone" (Baron and Fahmy 2009: 222). While it is good to be beneficent toward everyone, "one human being is closer to me than another" (MM 6:451). We have a duty of friendship (MM 6:469), and part of friendship is sharing more of one's friend's subjective ends than one shares with a stranger. I can use my judgment about which ends of others to adopt: It is "open to me to refuse them many things that they think will make them happy but that I do not" (MM 6:388). On the other hand, I cannot set ends for them on their behalf which are not their own:

> I cannot do good to anyone in accordance with my concepts of happiness (except to young children and the insane), thinking to benefit him by forcing a gift upon him; rather, I can benefit him only in accordance with *his* concepts [*Begriffen*] of happiness. (MM 6:454)

In this passage, Kant appears to be making the point that I can only benefit another in terms of his own concepts of happiness as a normative claim, but it is plausible to suppose that there is an implicit descriptive point here too – that others' subjective ends are individuated in terms of their own concepts of their ends. This point is central for my argument and will be discussed further below.

The problem in Kant's ethics that requires sympathy for its solution arises when the duty of beneficence is considered alongside an important thread in Kant's argument for moral rationalism. Kant holds that everyone must have the capacity to be motivated by the *same* moral reasons if morality is to have the kind of objectivity we must demand of it (CPrR 5:20). Transposed into the terminology of Kantian intentional teleology, the claim is that morality must involve objective ends (G 4:427), that is, ends which are ends for everyone, because they have a kind of value which everyone must recognize by virtue of their practical rationality, and are thus conatively grounded on pleasures, pains, and desires which everyone must have (G 4:460; CPrR 5:9 n, MM 6:212–3).

Kant argues that if reason *can* set its own ends, then we can have objective ends (G 4:427), because reason can cause pleasures, pains, and desires which everyone must have (G 4:461, MM 6:212–3). He argues that if reason *cannot* set its own ends, then our ends must be given to us in some other way, and the only other way in which ends can be given to us is empirically (CPrR 5:9 n, 5:21), by impacting our sensibility in such a way that pursuit of these ends gives pleasure or diminishes pain, and makes us happy (CPrR 5:21, 22, 25). However, with respect to sensibility, we each have a "specially constituted faculty of desire" (G 4:427). The things that empirically prompt desires and can thereby become empirically given ends for me may not empirically prompt desires for you and present themselves as empirically given ends for you. Thus empirically given ends are *subjective* ends, which Kant also calls "ends of inclination" (G 4:396), as well as "relative" and "material" ends (G 4:428). Their subjectivity implies that they are not intersubjectively available in the way objective ends must be (G 4:428). Kant concludes from this that reason must be able to set its own ends if morality is to have the kind of objectivity we must demand of it.

The problem to which rational sympathy is the solution comes into view when we consider the implications of this thread in Kant's argument for moral rationalism for our imperfect duty to adopt others' MPEs as our own. I ought to adopt others' MPEs, but others and I have differently constituted faculties of desire with respect to sensibility. This implies that I can only adopt others' MPEs if our sensibilities *contingently conform*, and this seems to force us to the conclusion that I *cannot* adopt their MPEs in the (presumably countless) cases in which our sensibilities do *not* conform. In Section 9, I argue that the theory of rational sympathy allows us to avoid this conclusion. Rational sympathy is a capacity to voluntarily *make* our contingent sensibilities conform in a way that suffices for adopting others' MPEs.

8 Responding to Exclusionists, and Distinguishing Adopting and Promoting Ends

Exclusionists are likely to object that the problem just claimed to be solved by rational sympathy is simply not a problem for Kant, because Kant has an account of how reason provides the motivation to be beneficent through respect for law alone in the *Groundwork* (G 4:423) and the second *Critique* (CPrR 5:34–5). In those texts, Kant's argument that we have a duty of beneficence involves reflection on a conflict between one's desire for one's own happiness and one's recognition of the universality of law. Commenting on G 4:423, Jens Timmermann gives a helpful account of this thread in Kant's thought:

> I notice someone I can easily help. At first my reaction is determined by the inevitable tendency to use what is mine exclusively for my own purposes. However, pure practical reason reminds me that it is impossible to will the selfish principle I am naturally tempted to act on as a universal law ... it makes me see that if I were justified in adopting a maxim of selfishness I would have to grant, on pain of contradiction, that everyone else facing the same choice would also be right to adopt the same maxim, which is precisely what I cannot coherently want. (Timmermann 2014: 135)

The exclusionist view is that the duty of beneficence which we discover in such reflection engages our feeling of respect for law, and thereby provides the only feeling and motivation we need for beneficence. But though such reflection suffices for demonstrating that we *have* a duty of beneficence, there are reasons to think that we cannot *fulfill* the duty thus demonstrated merely on the basis of the feeling of respect for law.

It is clear that Kant thinks the duty of beneficence requires us to promote (*befördern*) the ends of others (G 4:430, also see CPrR 5:34, MM 6:453, Eth-V 27:544 for similar language). But I can *promote* others' ends without *making them my own* if, as a means to different ends, I cause conditions that actualize their ends (as explained below). There is substantial evidence that the duty of beneficence also requires us to make others' ends our own (often labeled *adopting* their ends below).[20] At MM 6:450, Kant says the duty of beneficence can be "expressed as the duty to make others' *ends* my own [*Anderer ihre Zwecke zu den meinen zu machen*]." Similarly, at G 4:430, he writes that

> [T]he ends of a subject who is an end in itself must as far as possible be also *my* ends [*dessen Zwecke müssen … auch, so viel möglich, meine Zwecke sein*], if that representation is to have its *full* effect [*Wirkung*] in me.

Commentators have puzzled over what Kant means by "as far as possible" in this passage, in light of the latitude granted by the imperfect duty of beneficence (MM 6:393), and the interpretation offered below provides an explanation: Adopting another's end as my own through rational sympathy, rather than merely promoting it in the service of some other end, is a plausible way to understand *making it my own as far as possible*, as well as ensuring "its *full* effect in me." Another key text is MM 6:488:

> All moral relations of rational beings, which involve a principle of the harmony of the will of one with that of another, can be reduced [*zurückführen*] to *love* and *respect*; and … in the case of love the determining ground[t] of one's will

---

[20] Fahmy (2010: 314–327) also discusses the distinction between adopting and promoting others' ends. Fahmy focuses on the global end of the happiness of other people in general, while this book focuses on adopting MPEs of particular others. On Fahmy's interpretation, Kant thinks adopting this global end requires not just promoting it out of respect for law, but "cultivation of appropriate attitudes, feelings, and desires" (Fahmy 2010: 324) about the end which include feelings of love, and especially *Menschenliebe*, which Fahmy identifies with a distinctive feeling of benevolence. She argues that Kant's account of the "subjective conditions of receptiveness [*Empfänglichkeit*] to the concept of duty" (quoting Kant, MM 6:399) suggests that we should understand "love of human beings [*Menschenliebe*]" (quoting Kant, MM 6:401–2) as the "subjective condition of receptiveness to the duty to make the happiness of others one's end" (quoting Fahmy 2010: 326). This is an attractive and plausible interpretation. Fahmy sees sympathy as distinct from *Menschenliebe,* and holds that sympathy is not necessary for end-adoption (ibid., 327–8). I see sympathy as an aspect of *Menschenliebe,* and hold it is necessary for adopting MPEs.

[*Bestimmungsgrund des Willens*] can be reduced [*zurückführen*] to another's end [*Zweck*], and in the case of respect, to another's *right* [*Recht*]. (MM 6:488)

This passage is clearly relevant to beneficence, since it is a principle of harmony between wills, and it plausibly extends to sympathy as an aspect of love. The notion that the determining ground of one's will in relations of love can be *reduced* to another's end in beneficence suggests that the fundamental determining ground of one's will *just is the other's end,* and the idea of making the other's end the *Bestimmungsgrund* of *my* will suggests bringing that end *into* my will in a way which demands not just promotion but also adoption.

A concrete case can help clarify why Kant's intentional teleology implies that we must sympathize to adopt others' MPEs. Suppose my neighbor Abby has the MPE of adding an annex onto her ant farm. I can do things that promote this end (such as gluing boards) because I sympathize with her and thus have feelings which correspond to the pleasures and pains which are constituents of her desire to add the ant annex. This is promoting her end by adopting it. I can also promote the actualization of the ant annex from a variety of motivations which have nothing to do with sympathy: I can help (a) because I think her ant hobby is weird and funny, and by getting involved I can get details for a mocking story which will make Abby look ridiculous to others, or (b) because I want to cultivate a reputation of neighborliness. While I promote her end in both (a) and (b), I clearly do so as a *means* to ends which are *not* Abby's end, so these are not cases of adopting *her* end. The same is true if I help (c) because respect for law motivates me to promote her end in order to fulfill my duty of beneficence. Since the duty of beneficence gives me a reason to adopt as well as promote her end, I fail to do something I have a reason of beneficence to do in (c).

Exclusionists will find these claims about (a) and (b) unproblematic, but are likely to object when it comes to (c), since on their view motivation by respect for law suffices for all the moral motivation we need. They may ask why Kantians should care about the difference between adopting and promoting ends, given that promotion can actualize others' ends as well as adoption, and promotion for the sake of law is clearly a kind of moral motive. One reply is that Kantians should focus at least as much on the quality of our wills as they do on the consequences of our willing. Another reply is that Kant's remark at MM 6:488 (quoted above) implies that making another's end the *Bestimmungsgrund* of one's will is connected with a harmony of wills between agents that involves love *rather than* respect, and this suggests that failure to appreciate the distinction between adoption and promotion may deprive us of an opportunity to understand the role of love in Kant's intentional teleology. I think that what is manifested here is Kant's valuing of the care involved in a close engagement of wills. We can acknowledge that promoting others' ends out of respect for law is valuable, and still claim that something valuable is missing from such activity.

9 How Rational Sympathy Allows Adoption of Merely Permissible Ends

The necessary role of rational sympathy in actively adopting others' MPEs can be explained in more detail by beginning with a point mentioned in Section 7, that others' ends are individuated in terms of *their own concepts* of their ends. Kant may implicitly make this point in his normative claim that I can only benefit another in terms of his own concepts of happiness (MM 6:454). This point is also entailed by the only plausible interpretation of his explicit definitions of ends. At MM 6:384–5, Kant says that "[a]n end is an *object* of free choice, the representation of which determines it to an action (by which the object is brought about)." This gets clearer when connected with his definition at CPJ 5:220: "an end is the object of a concept insofar as the latter is regarded as the cause of the former." This is naturally read as implying that the concept (representation) of the end not only causes the end, but individuates it – the end *is* the end it is, as opposed to a different end, by virtue of the concept of the agent who has the end. Kant does not mention agents in these definitions, but once we acknowledge that ends are individuated by concepts, to whom could we suppose those concepts belong other than to the agents with the ends? If an end is individuated in terms of the concept of that end, then an end individuated in terms of a different concept would be a different end. This holds even if the same conditions actualize the end individuated with a different concept. These points are essential not only for Kant's intentional teleology but for any plausible intentional teleology.

Here is an example to explain and support these claims. Suppose I and my friends Oscar and C.M. are all seeking new household décor, though with different kinds of decorative objects in mind, and thus with differences in our ends. I have the end of *acquiring something made of glass*. Oscar embraces an anti-consumerist, repurposing ethic and thus has the end of *acquiring something discarded by another*. C.M. is preoccupied with alphabetization, and has the end of *acquiring something that starts with "C."* Suppose we spy a crystal ball in a dumpster outside a store suddenly vacated in the pandemic. Acquiring the crystal ball would actualize any of our ends, but our ends are nonetheless quite distinct, by virtue of the specific concepts included in our concepts of our ends. Kant sometimes calls such concepts *marks* (*Merkmale*) of concepts (B 114, A 241/B 299, CPrR 5:133, CPJ 20:277 n). This shows that to individuate our ends (to tell how they differ from other ends), it does not suffice to refer to the conditions of their actualization – we must also refer to our concepts of our ends. Since another's end is individuated by the other's concept of that end, I can only adopt the other's end in terms of the other's concept, since an effort to adopt it in terms of a different concept could only result in adopting a different end.

Kant's remarks at CPJ 5:220 and MM 6:384–5 (quoted above) imply that a concept of an end not only individuates that end but also causes that end to become actualized. At CPrR 5:9 n, CPJ 5:220, and MM 6:211, Kant makes it clear that this causation happens because that concept *motivates* us – because it engages with desires, which in turn requires engagement with pleasures and pains (though only insofar as we incorporate them – see e.g. Rel 6:24). Thus, adopting another's end requires not only that we acquire the concept individuating it in the sense of *understanding* it, but also in the sense of becoming *motivated* by it. There is no puzzle about how we can come to understand others' concepts in Kant's philosophy. Many of the concepts important in his philosophy are a priori, and do not vary between agents. Some of these are theoretical concepts, like *cause* or *substance*. Others are practical concepts, and some of these are concepts of ends, as in the formula of humanity, and our rationality entails that these concepts must connect with rational feelings such as respect for law, which ground rational desires and set objective ends for us. Empirical concepts are of course not a priori and must be acquired, and concepts of MPEs are typically empirical concepts. I may not have the concept of an ant annex until Abby shares it with me. Kant thinks that concepts are universally communicable, so Abby can communicate it to me. But having the concept, in the sense of understanding it, does not entail that I can adopt her end, because as an MPE, it may not connect with my contingent feelings of pleasure and pain, however rational I may be. This is just what it means for it to be an MPE. I must be able to *make* the concept of the MPE connect with my feelings if I am to adopt her MPE. We can learn more about what is required to make it connect if we consider two general features of the marks of MPE concepts, *marks of the first person*, and *marks of moral law*.

Concepts of MPEs often include *first-person indexicals*. Suppose that the concept which individuates Abby's ant annex end is the concept *building an annex onto **my** ant farm*. This may not be a necessary feature of MPE concepts, though there may be textual evidence that it is: Kant claims that "all material principles, which place the determining ground of choice in the pleasure or displeasure to be felt in the reality of some object ... belong without exception to the principle of **self**-love or **one's own** happiness" (CPrR 5:22, boldface added), and this may imply that all my MPE concepts contain marks of *me* or what I mean to be *mine*. If this is not a necessary feature of MPE concepts, it will often be a feature of them. To take Abby's end as my own in terms of her concept of her end, I must have a way to keep the indexical *indexed to her*, or I form a desire to add an annex to *my* ant farm rather than hers.

This point may seem to present a *reductio ad absurdum* of the claim that we ought to adopt other's ends in terms of their own concepts of their ends. However, Kant has a ready-made resolution in his theory of rational sympathy. Imaginatively putting myself in Abby's place lets me adopt Abby's end in terms of her concept while keeping the first-person indexical indexed to her. That is, the imagined subjective synthesis which provides the *form* of rational sympathy provides a first-person perspective indexed to Abby's first-person perspective, and the first-person indexicals in concepts tokened in thoughts framed in this imaginary perspective are thereby indexed to Abby rather than to me.

We cannot directly infer from the requirement for indexing preservation to a requirement for rational sympathy. As we saw earlier, Kant thinks we can step into others' perspectives in a heuristic way that does not involve sympathetic feeling, and heuristic perspective-taking may suffice for indexing-preservation. But indexing-preservation is only the first of two puzzles about adopting others' MPEs. The second puzzle is about *marks of law* included in concepts that individuate ends, and sympathetic rather than heuristic perspective-taking is required to solve it.

Consider the concept of *repaying my debt*. If I am practically rational, this concept includes a mark of *obligation*, since this is something I have a perfect duty to do. If I am motivated by respect for law, there is no puzzle about how I can have an end individuated by this concept – this concept engages with my motivation because of feelings made up of pleasures and pains which I necessarily have as a rational agent (G 4:460–1, CPrR 5:9 n, MM 6:211–2). Next, consider the concept of *caffeinating myself*. If this is a concept of an end for me, then insofar as I am a rational agent, the only mark of law it can contain for me is *permissibility*, because caffeination is a constituent of my happiness which is contingent from the perspective of rationality. This is just a long way of saying that it is an MPE. There is no puzzle about how *I* can be motivated by *my* MPEs. My concept of caffeinating myself contains no marks of law apart from permissibility, and I have innumerable permissible things I can do, so permissibility alone cannot give me a reason to caffeinate myself. But I experience the pleasures of being caffeinated and the pains of not being caffeinated despite their contingency, and it is because of them (and their incorporation) that caffeinating myself is an end for me.

However, the ends of others which I have an imperfect duty to adopt are often MPEs, and there is a puzzle about how *their* concepts of their MPEs can engage with *my* pleasures and pains so that their MPEs become ends for me. Abby's ant annex end is an MPE. She has this end because of features of her sensible nature which are contingent from the perspective of moral law. There is no puzzle about how *she* can be motivated by it, since her sensible nature presents it to her. The puzzle is about how *I* can be motivated by *her* MPE. The fact that her concept of her end has no mark of law apart from permissibility, and that I have innumerable permissible things I can do, means that permissibility cannot be a sufficient reason for me to set an end in terms of this concept – and crucially, it means that I cannot intelligibly set an end in terms of this concept *out of respect for law*, since there is simply (as it were) not enough law in the concept for that to be possible.

Since I have an imperfect duty to adopt her end, it is meritorious for me to adopt her end, so we might suppose that I can *add* a mark of merit to her concept in order to set her end for myself out of respect for law. But this is not possible. Her end is individuated by her concept, and since it is an MPE, she cannot rationally include a mark of merit in it. This means that a concept which includes a mark of merit would be a different concept, and would therefore individuate a different end.[21]

Since I cannot adopt her end as my own out of respect for law, I must look to the only other motivational source available in Kantian moral psychology, that is, my contingent pains and pleasures. I must have the capacity to voluntarily prompt pains and pleasures in myself which correspond to hers, so that her concept engages with my feelings in the way necessary for it to individuate an end for me. To do this, I must step into an imagined version of her perspective in a way that is rationally sympathetic, not merely logical and heuristic. When we communicate concepts with the goal of sharing feelings, we can draw on the productive imagination to populate the imagined manifold of sensibility we use to represent the other's perspective with imagined intuitional content, as

---

[21] This claim might seem to rely on implausibly fine individuation of ends. However, Kant's texts offer indirect but strong support for it. He emphasizes the importance of distinguishing ends I pursue for the sake of my happiness from ends which I pursue for the sake of duty, even in cases where I have a duty to care for my happiness. In the *Groundwork*, Kant states that "[t]o assure one's own happiness is a duty (at least indirectly); for, want of satisfaction with one's condition, under pressure from many anxieties and amid unsatisfied needs, could easily become a great *temptation to transgression of duty*" (G 4:399), and this might be taken to suggest that ends we set for the sake of happiness are sometimes moral ends too. But in the *Metaphysics of Morals*, Kant expands on this point by clarifying that it does *not* imply that "my natural and merely subjective end is thus made a duty," and that when we pursue happiness for the sake of avoiding "temptations to violate one's duty," then "the end is not the subject's happiness but his morality, and happiness is merely a means for removing obstacles" (MM 6:388). Kant's view that my subjective end of happiness is distinct from the end I pursue when I seek happiness from duty implies that I cannot add the mark of law to my subjective end of happiness without making it a different end. This generalizes to my adoption of another's subjective end of happiness, as well as the MPEs of which their happiness is the sum: if I add a mark of law apart from permissibility to their MPEs, I get different ends.

described in Section 6. When this communication is successful, it prompts us to have feelings like the other's feelings. Suppose Abby tells me that she grew up in an abusive household where, as a small child, she was sometimes locked in a closet all day, and her only companions were the ants marching through with crumbs from the kitchen, and that she consequently feels an unusual but steadfast dedication to all antkind. If I imagine being that lonely child in the cramped closet, and watching the lively ants trooping along, this provides intuitional content for the imaginary first-person perspective I use to represent Abby's experience, and insofar as I succeed, this allows me to "backtrack" from Abby's ant annex concept to sympathetic pleasures and pains that are enough like Abby's pleasures and pains to take her ant annex end, as individuated by her concept of it, as my own. If I do this voluntarily, with the attention and discipline needed to imagine vividly and accurately, and to regulate my feelings so as to avoid affect (which in this case might lead to awkward discomfort of the sort that tends toward alienation rather than connection), then I do this as a matter of rational sympathy.

Beneficence does not require us to *demand* such intimate communication with others. Sympathy is part of love and friendship, and Kant argues that love in friendship must be balanced by respect, and that respect sometimes requires us to limit our emotional engagement (e.g. MM 6:469–71). It makes sense to think that respect can require us to limit emotional engagement in relationships other than friendship. Abby may be uncomfortable sharing all the details that explain her dedication to ants, and if that is the case, it would be invasive of me to pry. Even if I am not able to share her feelings enough to *adopt* her end, I can still *promote* her end out of respect for law, and promotion is valuable even though it does not include everything of value in beneficence.

But suppose Abby *does* want to share her life story with me in enough detail for me to adopt her end. Once I imagine my way into her first-person perspective and acquire sympathetic feelings like the ones that motivate her, how should I act? Does interpreting end-adoption in terms of imaginative identification mean that I should continue to imagine that I am Abby when I act? Should I play-act *being* Abby, and grab all her tools as if they were mine, and get busy building the annex as if the real Abby were not standing there beside me? She might conceivably enjoy this, but she would probably find it a frustrating usurpation of her end. An interpretation of the duty of beneficence that encourages such usurpation would be problematic. However, the interpretation advocated here gives me *two* vantage points in my relationship with Abby. One is in my imagination, where I perform mental actions to identify with her and adopt her end. The other is in the real world, where I think of myself as a different person, and act bodily as well as mentally. It is my actions from the second vantage point which determine what I will do to contribute to actualizing her end. I need to maintain this duality of perspectives if I am to adopt Abby's end but also act helpfully in ways she will be happy about. To provide such help, the end I set from my ordinary, unimagined vantage point will need to be *different* than Abby's end: My end should be to *support* Abby in her pursuit of her end. My pursuit of this end does not devolve into promotion of her end out of respect for law, because it is motivated by the sympathetic feelings I draw from my imaginative vantage point. What motivates me to support her is still rational sympathy. But the end at which I aim from my ordinary vantage point is nonetheless a different end. Abby's end may include doing all the building herself, and it may be that the only means I can usefully take toward my end of supporting her in pursuit of her end is to bring her a glass of iced tea (or perhaps lemonade, if she does not enjoy caffeinating herself).[22]

10 Sages and Sympathy in Kant's Theory of Friendship

Kant's remarks on friendship provide crucial evidence for the interpretation of sympathy presented here. In the Vigilantius Ethics text supporting the distinction between rational and natural sympathy, Kant argues that friends can share moral rather than instinctual sympathy when they employ reason to communicate accurately and sympathize correctly (Sections 2 and 3). Both the Vigilantius Ethics and the Metaphysics of Morals suggest that friends' sympathy involves imaginative projection into one another's perspectives (Section 5). However, a number of texts on friendship suggest sharp limits to the role sympathy should play in an ideally moral life. The Kantian sage can appear to reject sympathetic suffering when his friend suffers and he can do nothing to alleviate the suffering. Since Kant presents the sage as a moral ideal to which we should aspire, he can appear to suggest that we should all feel this way. This view seems *uncaring* to many commentators. The next few sections argue that we should not attribute this view to Kant. Kant is committed to the view that both sages and ordinary people must suffer in sympathy with friends even when they cannot help, because sympathy is necessary to adopt others' MPEs, and we ought to take friends' MPEs as our own. The sage rejects affective excesses of natural sympathy, but not rational sympathy.

---

[22] My thoughts here have been helped by Fahmy's distinction between two ways of interpreting the idea of sharing in another's ends, which she calls the *identical* and *nonidentical ends* interpretations (Fahmy 2016). She argues that we should prefer the nonidentical ends interpretation, because the identical ends interpretation threatens to license end-usurpation (2016: 158–162). However, Kant's remarks do suggest an identical ends approach, and my interpretation seeks to make this approach plausible. The usurpation threat is defused via the two vantage points: I have an end identical to the other's in my vantage point in imagination, and a nonidentical end in my vantage point in the real world. This yields a hybrid of the identical and nonidentical ends interpretations.

Commentators have often drawn on Kant's theory of friendship as a defense against the objection that his moral theory is too emotionally detached to properly value particular interpersonal connections of feeling. Kant entitles the conclusion of the *Doctrine of Virtue* "On the most intimate union of love with respect in friendship," and writes that

> *Friendship* (considered in its perfection) is the union of two persons through equal mutual love and respect ... this is an ideal of each sympathizing with and communicating[t] about the other's wellbeing [*Ideal der Theilnehmung und Mittheilung an dem Wohl eines jeden*] through the morally good will that unites them, and even though it does not produce the complete happiness of life, the adoption of this ideal in their disposition toward each other makes them deserving of happiness; hence human beings have a duty of friendship. (MM 6:469)

Remarks like this also appear in a number of Kant's lectures. According to Collins' Ethics notes, to "possess such a friend, of whom I know that his disposition is upright and kindly, neither malicious nor false ... [t]his is the whole purpose of man, which allows him to enjoy his existence" (Eth-C 27:427). On the basis of such passages, Christine Korsgaard writes that "[t]o become friends is to create a neighborhood where the Kingdom of Ends is real" (Korsgaard 1996: 194). We might also say that the way friendship correlates valuable dispositions of friends toward one another with their shared enjoyment of life makes friendship a fragment of the highest good which is accessible within experience. At least since Herbert Paton (1956), and increasingly in recent years,[23] commentators have directed proponents of the detachment objection to Kant's theory of friendship.

However, the cold (*kalt*) and indifferent (*gleichgültig*) attitude attributed to the grieving philanthropist (G 4:398) appears again in passages on friendship, in connection with Kant's *sage*, who he sometimes also calls the *stoic* or *wise man*. The sage is not a "finite *holy* [being] (who could never be tempted to violate duty)," but rather a human being who has "*autocracy* of practical reason," that is, mastery of "one's inclinations when they rebel against the law" (MM 6:383). The sage serves as "an ideal (to which one must continually approximate)" (ibid.).

The earliest passage is in Herder's Ethics notes (1762–64):

> Indifference [*Gleichgültigkeit*], as a moral quality, is the opposite of human love; but even by this cold-bloodedness [*Kaltblütigkeit*] I may understand a very good trait, if it holds the love inspired by sympathy [*Sympathie*] in check, and gives it the right degree[t] [*rechten Grad*]. If the sympathetic

---

[23] See for example, Baron (1995, 2013), Baxley (2010), Denis (2000), Fahmy (2009, 2010), Sherman (1997), Varden (2020a, 2020b), and Wood (1999, 2008).

inclinations [*Theilnehmende Neigungen*] are blind and serve no purpose, the stoic must say: If you cannot be of help to others, then what business is it of yours, pray? (Eth-H 27:54)

This passage does not explicitly address friendship, but Herder's notes go on to address friendship immediately afterwards (ibid.), suggesting an endorsement of indifference toward friends we cannot help too.

The second passage is in Collins' Ethics notes (1784):

If I now observe such a man sitting in misery^t, and see that I have no way of altering it, and cannot come to his aid in any fashion, I may turn away coldly [*kalt*] and say, with the Stoic: What is it to me? My wishes [*Wünsche*] cannot help him. But so far as I can extend a hand to help him, I am to that extent able to promote [*befördern*] his happiness, and sympathize [*Antheil*] with his plight; but I show no sympathy whatever for his plight in harbouring ardent^t wishes for his deliverance. (Eth-C 27:421)

Here too we have no direct reference to friendship, but once again a discussion of friendship immediately follows (Eth-C 27:422). So here too Kant can seem to hold that if I cannot help a suffering friend, I need not experience any sympathetic pain.

The most famous remarks on this theme appear in the *Doctrine of Virtue* (1787):

It was a sublime way of thinking that the Stoic ascribed to his wise man when he had him say "I wish for a friend, not that he might help *me* in poverty, sickness, imprisonment, etc., but rather that I might stand by *him* and rescue a human being." But the same wise man, when he could not rescue his friend, said to himself "what is it to me?" In other words, he rejected compassion [*Mitleidenschaft*] ... In fact, when another suffers and, although I cannot help him, I let myself be infected [*anstecken*] by his pain (through my imagination), then two of us suffer, though the trouble really (in nature) affects only *one*. But there cannot possibly be a duty to increase the ills in the world and so to do good *from compassion* [*Mitleid*]. (MM 6:457)

This passage can also seem to assert the view that if I cannot help my suffering friend, I need not suffer in sympathy. Though I am in the company of readers who find this view distressing, I do not wish to claim that it is obviously false. Utilitarians, for example, could endorse it. However, if it is in fact the view we should attribute to Kant, then Kant's theory of friendship offers only a partial defense against the detachment objection. This is likely to become increasingly damaging to the reception of Kant's ethics as contemporary ethics makes the value of care more central.[24] I take it to be essential to our intuitive understanding of care that it hurts when someone we care about suffers, and that we can

---

[24] Others who have discussed Kant from the perspective of care ethics include Hay (2013), Sarah Clark Miller (2012), Paytas (2015), Varden (2020a, 2020b), and Wood (1999, 2008).

only banish that suffering if we stop caring. If Kant's advice is that we may stop caring when we cannot help a suffering friend, then the detachment objection may be insurmountable. Reading Kant's theory of friendship through the lens of his theory of rational sympathy gives us reasons to think this is not his advice.

The interpretation of sages and friendship presented below builds on a line of thought developed in the work of Marcia Baron and Lara Denis. Baron argues that Kant's central theme in the passages about friendship and the sage is not to advocate the *absence* of sympathetic feeling, but rather the ability to *voluntarily regulate* it, emphasizing Kant's *Empfindsamkeit/Empfindelei* distinction (discussed in Sections 2 and 4). She thinks Kant nonetheless attributes to the sage the ability to "turn off" sympathetic pain "if it does no good" (1995: 216), and that Kant approves of the sage's exercise of it when she cannot help. Baron thinks that if Kant is to properly value care, then Kant's ethics must be corrected so that it values sympathetic suffering even when we cannot help, and so that it advocates sensitive moderation of sympathy in such cases rather than the cessation of sympathy (1995: 221).

Denis argues that fine-grained analysis of Kant's texts shows that he *already* holds the views that Baron thinks Kant must adopt, so that no correction is required. She notes that Kant says the sage exemplifies a virtue he calls *apathy* (*Apathie*), such that the "wise man [*Weise*] must never be in a state of affect [*Affect*], not even in that of compassion [*Mitleids*] with the misfortune of his best friend" (AP 7:253, Denis 2000: 51–52). *Apathie* does not mean "lack of feeling [*Fühllosigkeit*]" but rather "absence of affects [*Affectlosigkeit*]" (Kant MM 6:408, Denis ibid.). As mentioned above in Section 2, Denis shows that Kant's treatment of the concept of *cold-bloodedness* involves a similar distinction. Kant says that *frigidity* [*Kaltsinnigkeit*] is a "want of love" and a "lack of the feeling whereby the state of others affects us," while "cold-bloodedness [*Kaltblütigkeit*] is a want of affect [*Affekts*] in love, and that "cold-bloodedness [*Kaltblütigkeit*] of love^t provides regularity and order" (Eth-C 27:420, Denis 2000: 53). Denis argues that this shows that an apathetic, cold sage *does* have sympathy for suffering friends she cannot help – she simply ensures that it does not prompt affect (Denis 2000: 53–55). Denis does not discuss Eth-H 27:54 (quoted above), where Kant claims that *Gleichgültigkeit* can be a "moral quality" and a "good trait," but her interpretation encourages attention to how it functions when it serves as a good trait: It gives the love inspired by sympathy the "right degree [*rechten Grad*]" (ibid.). Perhaps Kant thinks we have a capacity to be indifferent (perhaps fully possessed only by sages) which allows us to dampen sympathy to zero, but these passages provide strong evidence that he thinks its *moral* role is to regulate sympathy rather than to eliminate it, so that we sympathize rationally rather than naturally.

Denis does not connect sympathy to the intentional teleology of beneficence in the way this Element does, but this connection allows us to expand on her interpretation in a way that may be congenial to her overall view. Denis reads Kant as holding that it may be psychologically impossible for actual human beings to completely suppress sympathy when they cannot help, once they have become sympathetically engaged with their friends in the way they have a duty to strive to be. She thinks this gives us grounds to worry that any actual human beings who are able to entirely suppress sympathy for their purported friends have never really become sympathetically engaged with them in this way, and that they may never really have adopted their purported friends' ends as their own (Denis 2000: 64–66).

I extend this thought with the argument that sympathy is necessary for adopting others' MPEs, not only as a matter of empirical psychology, but also as a matter of practical rationality. The next two sections apply this argument to suffering with friends when we cannot help. My friend's end of *making my pain stop* is an MPE. If her pain is intense, then this end will be weighty and constant in her mind, but she is vulnerable to pain because she has a sensible nature which is contingent from the perspective of moral law, and so her pain is not in itself morally bad (CPrR 5:60). Since it is an MPE, I can only cease sympathizing with her suffering if I cease to adopt her end. But I ought not to cease to adopt her end.

It may be objected that this argument fails because of what Kant calls the "latitude" in the imperfect duty to adopt others' ends: This duty tells us we must adopt some ends of some others, but it does not tell us that we must adopt all of anyone's ends. So it might seem that I can refuse to adopt my friend's MPE of *making my pain stop* and remain ethically unblemished as long as I adopt other ends of my friend. The problem with this objection is that the duty of friendship is regulated by an ideal of sharing all our ends and all our feelings.

11 Friendship as an Ideal of Sharing All Our Ends and All Our Feelings

This section argues that the ideal of friendship includes maximal sharing of feelings and maximal sharing of ends, and then poses a question about the nature of the correlation between these maxima which Kant's theory of sympathy helps answer. The distinction between natural and rational sympathy is not always relevant in this section and is thus referenced only where necessary.

It is a characteristic mark of Kantian ideals that they contain maxima (OP 21:30, also see Anth-F 25:609, Met-L2 28:555, Eth-C 27:247). At MM 6:469 Kant says that we must strive for friendship "as a maximum of good disposition

[*Gesinnung*] toward each other" (MM 6:469). Vigilantius' Ethics notes make clear that that this involves a maximum of shared feelings: Kant says that in the ideal of friendship, "each mutually sympathizes^t [*teilnehmen*] with **every** situation of the other, as if it were encountered by himself" (Eth-V 27:677, boldface added). This maximum is probably not well-understood as a maximum of *intensity* of feeling. I should feel as if I encountered my friend's situations myself. Even if I should match the intensity of her feelings when I can do so without affect, she presumably rarely experiences feelings of maximal intensity. The maximum instead appears to be one of *extension*, since it extends to all my friend's situations.

Kant emphasizes caution in implementing this aspect of the ideal in actual friendships. He thinks we are driven to friendship not only by duty but also by a need to "*reveal* [ourselves] to others." However, friends should aim at "complete confidence ... in revealing their secret judgments and feelings to each other" only insofar as such revelations are consistent with mutual respect and prudence (MM 6:469–71). Friendships in the actual world are constrained by asymmetries of attachment: If my friend concludes that I love her more than she loves me, she may lose respect for me, so I must constrain my sympathetic attachment. Furthermore, if I share feelings that reflect badly upon me, for example, an unreasonable resentment for a third party, then I may not only lose her respect – I may also place myself in jeopardy if our friendship ends and she uses my feelings against me. In this vein, Kant comments that "[e]ven to our best friend, we must not discover ourselves as we naturally are and know ourselves to be, for that would be a nasty business" (Eth-C 27:427).[25] But this passage is about the best friend Kant thinks we can hope to have in the world as it is, not the ideal best friend. Both my need and my duty compel me to search for friends with whom I can closely embody the ideal: "Pure sincerity in friendship can be no less required of everyone even if up to now there may never have been a sincere friend" (G 4:408).[26] Kant may be too skeptical in his dim view of the prospects for actual friendships that closely conform to the ideal, but even if he is correct, this view is not in conflict with the claim that the ideal of friendship is an ideal of sharing all feelings.

We should also read Kant as holding that the ideal of friendship includes a maximum of adopting all one's friend's permissible ends. We have a universal

---

[25] Additional constraints would be needed in a complete account. For example, even if Abby becomes my friend, and she is certain that sharing her childhood sorrow will not diminish my love or be used against her, she may feel that bringing such a deep shared sorrow into our friendship will make it difficult to continue the friendship.

[26] Helga Varden connects the fragility of friendship to Kant's notion of *unsocial sociability* and highlights the importance of unity between friends and moderation of affect in friendship (2020a: 66–71).

imperfect duty to take others' ends as our own (G 4:430, MM 6:450), but Kant acknowledges that "one human being is closer to me than another" (MM 6:451) and that our friends are our closest others, and this makes it intuitive to think that we have a special duty to adopt our friends' ends.[27] It is natural to think that striving for a "maximum of good disposition toward each other" (MM 6:470) requires us to adopt more of our friends' ends as we become closer, striving toward adoption of all their permissible ends. Kant says this in fairly clear detail with respect to friends' *needs* (*Bedürfnisse*). In the Collins Ethics, Kant says that "[t]he friendship of need is that whereby the participants may entrust each other with a reciprocal concern in regard to their needs in life," and that "we must presuppose" this kind of friendship "in every friendship."[28] He says that "I must ... have confidence in each of my true friends, that he would be able and willing to look after my affairs, and promote my interests" – "my friend is ... ready to aid me **in any difficulty**" (Eth-C 27:424–6, boldface added). According to the Vigilantius Ethics, "[f]riends ... undertake to support one another in their needs with **all their powers and means**" (Eth-V 27:684; boldface added). It might seem that our needs are only a subset of our ends, while happiness includes all our ends, but in fact, Kant understands happiness as a need (CPrR 5:110, also see MM 6:393). So these passages provide strong support for the thesis we ought to adopt all our friends' permissible ends as our own. Here too the maximum we find is one of extension.

Kant sees this aspect of the ideal of friendship as constrained by actuality for reasons like those for constraining sympathy. Power and wealth are often asymmetrical between friends, so accepting "a favor from the other" can lead favor-givers to take on the status of benefactors, and can lead beneficiaries to lose respect in their own eyes as well as in those of the benefactors (MM 6:471). However, actual constraints on maximal end-taking do not conflict with the claim that the ideal includes maximal end-taking. Thus, the most plausible view to attribute to Kant is as follows. I must strive to adopt all my friend's ends, but it is rational for me to prioritize our shared end of preserving our friendship, because of the way I am essentially involved in this end of my friend. If my friend can achieve her other ends without my help, and my help would threaten our friendship, I do not help her achieve her other ends. On the other hand, if she cannot achieve her other ends without my help, and those ends are more important to her than our friendship, then I help, despite the threat. Kant's point about the hazards of favors is thereby made compatible with his view that we ought to adopt all our friends' permissible ends as our own.

---

[27] See Hay (2013: 59–60) for a discussion of the preferential treatment of intimates.
[28] Paton (1956: 55) and Baron (2013: 374) emphasize this point.

When we see correlated maxima, as we do between sharing ends and sharing feelings in the ideal of friendship, it is helpful to inquire about the nature of the correlation. Is Kant making a normative claim that we *should* share more feelings as we share more ends, or claiming that, as a matter of fact, we actually *do?* If the latter, is the correlation (1) a correlation with exceptions, such that we will sometimes find cases of sharing ends without sharing feelings?[29] Or is the correlation (2) the consequence of laws of empirical psychology which govern all actual human beings and make it psychologically impossible for actual people to adopt others' ends without sharing their feelings?[30] Or could the correlation be (3) a conceptual necessity of Kant's practical philosophy, so that looking for people who adopt others' ends without sympathizing turns out to be looking for a conceptual impossibility? If (1), then actual human beings could adopt suffering friends' ends without suffering in sympathy. If (2), then perhaps we can imagine that the sage, as an unactualized ideal with perfect rational control of her feelings, could accomplish this feat, even though actual humans cannot. If (3), then neither actual humans nor sages can adopt suffering friends' ends without suffering in sympathy.

According to the account of sympathy presented here, (3) is the right way to understand the correlation, at least with respect to others' MPEs. My friend's end of *stopping my pain* is an MPE. I may do things to alleviate her pain because (I) I adopt her end through rational sympathy, (II) I want to sleep soundly and her groans wake me, or (III) it is a way of fulfilling my duty of beneficence. As explained in Section 8, while I promote her end in all these ways, and there may be no differences in the consequences I produce, I promote her end as a means to different ends in cases (II) and (III), neither of which are *her* end. Since sympathy is a necessary condition of adopting others' MPEs, we can only cease suffering in sympathy with our friends if we cease to adopt some of the ends they care about most, and we thereby forsake our friends in an important sense. Though we do not withhold help, since there is no help we can provide, we nonetheless withhold care. We might say that we forsake our friends in our hearts. Since we ought not to forsake our friends, we ought to suffer in sympathy even when we cannot help. This holds not only for ordinary people but also for sages. Sages are different from ordinary people in that they are able to exercise perfect rational control over their feelings. But as idealized human beings, they

---

[29] Recent advocates of views which I take to entail this include Paytas (2015), Thomason (2017), and Timmermann (n.d.).

[30] This view is suggested by Denis (2000: 64–66), though she does not claim that there is no conceptual necessity at work. Guyer may hold the view that there is an empirical necessity but no conceptual necessity: he claims that "the role and indeed the number and kinds of moral feelings involved in the phenomenal etiology of moral action can be decided on empirical grounds **and only such**" (2010: 132, boldface added).

too must sympathetically step into others' perspectives to adopt others' MPEs.[31] It would seem that even God cannot adopt others' MPEs without sympathy, so if God lacks sympathy (and CPrR 5:34 suggests Kant thinks this), then only beings like us can adopt others' MPEs. This casts light on the special role we play in the moral world.

12 Four Objections to the Rationally Sympathetic Interpretation of Friendship

Let us consider four objections to the interpretation of sympathy in friendship just presented. First, in Friedländer's Anthropology lecture notes, Kant can appear to suggest that we should not sympathize with suffering friends we cannot help because it makes things more difficult for them: "[I]f you cannot help him at all ... then go away unperturbed. Weeping, mourning, lamenting ... make the other's misfortune more acute and unbearable for him" (Anth-F 25:612).[32] It is clear that someone rationally sympathizing would not experience or express her sympathetic pain in the unmoderated ways depicted in this remark. The interpretation presented here thus makes it reasonable to suppose that Kant's concern in this passage is just that affect-driven excesses of *natural* sympathy can distress the suffering friend. Admittedly, even moderated expressions of rational sympathy could probably be distressing sometimes. In some cases this problem could be resolved by sympathizing without communicating one's sympathy.[33] But suppose my friend wishes to communicate to confirm that I am not sympathizing. She may say that she will rest easier if she knows I have stopped thinking of her pain with sorrow – that she cares more about my living a joyful life than she does about my sympathy. This now appears to be

---

[31] Kant depicts the sage as "raising himself above the animal nature of the human being" (CPrR 5:127), and if the sage is an ideal for us, then we should strive to raise ourselves above animality too. But what this raising consists in is a matter of debate. The greater the distance from animality we take it to demand, the greater the tension becomes between this ideal and an ideal which Helga Varden shows is suggested by Rel 6:26–8. Since animality, humanity, and personality all have predispositions to the good, it seems ideal to embody a synthesis of all three (Varden 2020a: 29–38, 66, 171). As noted earlier, Kant thinks sympathy is something we share with animals, and gives the example that "when a pig is butchered ... the others scream" (Anth-F 25:576; also see Eth-V 27:671, Eth-Mr 29:626). He also associates the human experience of natural sympathy with our animality (Anth-F 25:607). According to the present interpretation, rational sympathy does not involve feelings which are qualitatively different from those of natural sympathy – it involves rational regulation of those feelings. We might say that the threads of feeling out of which rational sympathy is woven are no different from the threads of our natural, animal sympathy. This suggests that when sages rationally sympathize, they raise themselves above animal sympathy only in the sense of rationally transforming it. This diminishes the tension between the ideal of the sage and the ideal suggested by Rel 6:26–8.
[32] See Hurter et al. (2014) for empirical evidence that this phenomenon sometimes occurs.
[33] Fahmy (2009) correctly emphasizes the role of sympathy in communication for Kant, but this kind of case shows that the value of sympathy cannot lie exclusively in communication.

a case where there *is* something I can do to help – I can help her pursue one of her ends, that I live a joyous life – but according to the interpretation defended here, I can only do this by relinquishing her end of stopping her pain, in the sense of ceasing to adopt it (though I should still search for ways to promote it). In such a case, the best I can do is to adopt some but not all of her ends. The world constrains the actualization of ideals.

Some may raise a second objection – that Kant endorses *utilitarianism* when it comes to sympathetic suffering. Kant says that "when another suffers and, although I cannot help him, I let myself be infected [*anstecken lasse*] by his pain, then two of us suffer, though the trouble really (in nature) affects only *one*," and proceeds to say that "there cannot possibly be a duty to increase the ills in the world" (MM 6:457, also see a similar argument at Anth-Mr 25:1321). He can appear to be invoking the utilitarian argument that there is no moral reason to experience pain unless that pain is outweighed by its diminution of some other pain. But Kant is typically understood to be an opponent of utilitarian thinking, and while this sometimes leads to oversimplifications of his moral views, we should be cautious about attributing utilitarian arguments to him. So it is important to carefully consider the particular terms Kant uses to explain what I do not have a duty to do in this case. He says I have no duty to *let his pain infect* (*anstecken lasse*) me. Kant uses an adjectival form of *anstecken* earlier on the very same page of the *Doctrine of Virtue* to characterize what he calls "*humanitas aesthetica*," which was shown to be a term for natural sympathy rather than rational sympathy. Kant explains the sense in which *humanitas aesthetica* is "communicable" by saying that it is "like receptivity to ... infectious[t] diseases [*ansteckender Krankheiten*]" (MM 6:457). *Ansteckung* and its derivatives appear rarely in Kant's corpus, so this connection between passages in close proximity means we should read Kant as claiming that we have no duty to sympathize naturally with a suffering friend who we cannot help, but *not* claiming that we have no duty to sympathize rationally.

The third objection is based on a passage in Collins' Ethics notes which appears in close proximity to the story of the sage, part of which we saw earlier, in which Kant can seem to be criticizing sympathy for friends we cannot help because it is a *mere wish*:

> I show no sympathy whatever for his plight in harbouring ardent[t] wishes [*sehnliche Wünsche*] for his deliverance. The heart ... is only a good heart insofar as it is able to contribute something to the other's happiness, and not when it merely wishes [*nur ... wünscht*] for that ... People think here that sympathy [*Theilnehmung*] for another's fate[t] [*Schicksaal*], and kindness of heart, consist merely in feelings [*Gefühl*] and wishes. Yet he who pays no heed at all to the wretchedness of others, where he can be of no help, and who

is indifferent [*gleichgültig*] to all misfortune that cannot be altered, but takes trouble only where he can do something and be of help, is in fact a practical man. (Eth-C 27:421–2)

The first thing to note in interpreting this passage is Kant's specification in the first sentence that he is criticizing *sehnliche* ("ardent") wishes.[34] The word *sehnliche* seems to appear exclusively as a modifier for *Wünsche* ("wishes") in Kant's corpus, in three different versions of students' notes from Kant's Ethics lectures (the other appearances are at Eth-Mr 27:1543 and Eth-B 253). "Ardent" suggests that Kant is specifically criticizing affect-driven wishes that involve natural sympathy. Additional support for this reading comes from interpretative points discussed earlier. According to Herder's Ethics notes, *Gleichgültigkeit* is a "good trait" only insofar as it "holds sympathy in check and gives it the right degree" (Eth-H 27:54). In light of the interpretation advanced here, we can say that *Gleichgültigkeit* is a good trait only insofar as we draw on it to experience rational sympathy rather than natural sympathy. Herder's Ethics notes identify the good sort of *Gleichgültigkeit* with *Kaltblütigkeit* ("cold-bloodedness"). We should also recall the Collins Ethics distinction between *Kaltsinnigkeit* ("frigidity") and *Kaltblütigkeit*, which defines the former as a "want of love," and the latter as a "want of *Affekts* in love" which "provides regularity and order" in love. That distinction appears at Eth-C 27:420, in the paragraph *immediately prior* to the Eth-C 27:421–2 criticism of mere wishing currently under discussion. Together these points provide evidence that the *Gleichgültigkeit* Kant recommends at Eth-C 27:422 as an alternative to the sympathy of mere wish is not a state devoid of sympathetic feeling, but rather a *kaltblütig* state of *regular, orderly sympathy in the right degree*. We should hold that he is criticizing *natural* sympathy as mere wish, but *endorsing* something like wishing which involves rational sympathy.

It may seem puzzling to claim that there is room for such a distinction. Can Kantian ethics accommodate a distinction between (i) mere wish, which is morally empty and should be eradicated, (ii) a kind of conative state which is *like* wishing in that it produces no useful action but is nonetheless morally valuable, and (iii) the kind of conative state that produces useful action? The answer is yes – Kant unequivocally relies on such a threefold distinction in the *Groundwork*'s famous "useless jewel" passage, in which he argues that goodness of will does not entail good actions:

> Even if, by a special disfavor of fortune ... this [good] will should wholly lack the capacity to carry out its purpose – if with its greatest efforts it should yet achieve nothing and only the good will were left (not, of course, as a mere

---

[34] The Cambridge translation renders *sehnliche* as "passionate," but given that "passion" is typically used as a translation for Kant's technical term *Leidenschaft*, I use "ardent" instead.

wish [*bloßer Wunsch*] but as the summoning of all means insofar as they are in our control) – then, like a jewel, it would still shine by itself, as something that has its full worth in itself. Usefulness or fruitlessness can neither add anything to this worth nor take anything away from it. (G 4:394)

This pivotal passage entails a threefold distinction between (i) mere wish, (ii) a kind of conative state which "achieve[s] nothing" but is nonetheless morally valuable because it is an activity of practical reason, and involves the "summoning all of all means insofar as they are in our control," and (iii) a kind of conative state which is based on practical rationality and leads to useful action. Kant implies that both (ii) and (iii) are sources of moral worth, though (i) is not. Kant's assertion that there is moral value in (ii)-type cases is fundamental for understanding the sense in which his ethics is non-consequentialist.[35] That is, to recognize the value in (ii)-type cases is to recognize that the value of the *activity of good willing* is independent of the value of the *states of affairs* it sometimes brings into being. We can draw a distinction between (i)- and (ii)-type cases of sympathizing when one cannot help which corresponds to the distinction between rational and natural sympathy. When, in rational sympathy, we wrack our brains to try to find ways to help, sifting through our knowledge of empirical laws to find relevant hypothetical imperatives we might follow, we are clearly summoning means. When we voluntarily and sympathetically put ourselves in the other's place to understand the help they need, we are summoning means here too, and the text supports this claim: In §34 of the *Doctrine of Virtue,* Kant tells us that "*humanitas practica,*" which was shown above to be rational sympathy, involves using our "receptivity" to "[s]*ympathetic joy* and *sadness* ... **as a means** to promoting active and rational benevolence" (MM 6:456), and repeats the point in §35: We should "cultivate the compassionate ... feelings" and "make use of them **as so many means** to sympathy based on moral principles" (MM 6:457, my boldface). Rational sympathy is not the passive feeling-state which Kant criticizes as mere wish – it is an *action* of the mind and will which has as much claim to being a (ii)-type activity as anything in Kant's ethics, and thus has the credential we need to recognize it as an aspect of goodwill.

The fourth and final objection is that the claim that we ought to adopt friends' ends even when we cannot help runs afoul of the "ought implies can" principle. How can I have a duty to adopt an end which I cannot promote? The distinction between adoption and promotion and the distinction between (ii)- and (iii)-type cases demonstrate that there is more to adoption of an end through rational sympathy than is involved in promotion. It is a mental action which can be

---

[35] MM 6:451–2 also suggests that wishes are not morally empty in the context of benevolence. Thanks to Melissa Seymour Fahmy for suggesting this point.

recognized as having moral worth even when it does not lead to useful consequences. Adopting an end is something we can *do* even when we cannot promote the end, and it creates a rational connection of care which Kantians should acknowledge to be intrinsically valuable in the same way that rational agency itself is intrinsically valuable.

13 Sympathy as a Moral Incentive, and Its Relationship to Respect

A key motivation for this Element's inclusive approach to sympathy is to show that sympathy can have standing as a moral incentive alongside respect for law, despite Kant's claim in the *Critique of Practical Reason* that respect for law is "the sole ... moral incentive" (CPrR 5:78, also see 5:81, 85). The preceding text offers support for this view, but sometimes indirectly or implicitly. This section argues for this claim more directly.[36]

An incentive (*Triebfeder*) is a "subjective determining ground of the will [*Bestimmungsgrund des Willens*] of a being whose reason does not by its nature necessarily conform with the objective law" (CPrR 5:72, also see 5:75). Incentives can be pathological or moral (5:85, Anth 7:253). Pathological incentives are based on inclinations and feelings which are contingent from the perspective of law (G 4:411). In moral incentives, "the incentive ... can never be anything other than the moral law": The "objective determining ground" of finite rational wills is "also the subjectively sufficient determining ground" (CPrR 5:72). The objective determining ground becomes a subjective determining ground through our own free activity: We *make* the law an incentive through practical reasoning which both changes our contingent pleasures and pains feelings and also prompts new, rational pleasures and pains (5:71–89; 5:116–7). Kant refers to both the law *and* the rationally transformed feelings we prompt in ourselves as moral incentives (5:78), but emphasizes that we must keep these feelings' free, rational etiology in mind to understand them as moral incentives (5:76).

A remark in the *Metaphysics of Morals* suggests a short but strong argument for the claim that rational sympathy is a moral incentive:

> Pleasure that must precede one's observance of the law in order for one to act in conformity with the law is pathological and one's conduct follows the *order of nature;* but pleasure that must be *preceded* by the law in order to be felt is in the *moral order.* (MM 6:378)

What makes it possible for us to sympathize rationally rather than merely naturally is the regulation of our sympathetic pleasures and pains by practical

---

[36] Correspondence with Owen Ware was helpful in refining the arguments in this section.

rationality, which is intrinsically law-governed. Rationally sympathetic pleasures and pains must in this way be preceded by the law. The distinction drawn in this passage thus implies that rationally sympathetic pleasures are in the moral order, and it is intuitive to think that the same would hold for sympathetic pains. This passage does not state that feelings in the moral order are moral incentives, but it is intuitive to read it this way. Another passage from the *Metaphysics of Morals* (also discussed in Section 8) supports this reading:

> All moral relations of rational beings, which involve a principle of the harmony of the will of one with that of another, can be reduced [*zurückführen*] to *love* and *respect*; and ... in the case of love the determining ground^t of one's will [*Bestimmungsgrund des Willens*] can be reduced [*zurückführen*] to another's end [*Zweck*] (MM 6:488).

A moral incentive is a moral determining ground of one's will (CPrR 5:72). If the determining ground of one's will in moral relations of love (of which sympathy is an aspect) is another's end, then the manifestations in the feeling of the activity of making another's end the determining ground of one's will can also be understood as moral incentives. Since this activity is rational sympathy, the feelings it involves can be understood as moral incentives.

A longer argument addressing the relationship between sympathy and respect may also be helpful. Kant's most detailed account of the nature and moral-psychological role of respect is in the *Critique of Practical Reason*. His claim there that respect is the sole moral incentive must be balanced by his emphasis on its free, rational etiology: It is not how respect *feels* that makes it an incentive, but instead the way it manifests the free, rational activity of willing lawfully. Thus his fundamental claim in the *Critique of Practical Reason* is that the feeling of respect is the *unique manifestation* of this activity. Kant does not make any such uniqueness claim in the *Metaphysics of Morals*. There, Kant tells us that there are multiple feelings which are "subjective conditions of receptiveness to the concept of duty" which "lie at the basis of morality," including "*moral feeling, conscience, love* of one's neighbor, *and respect* for oneself" (MM 6:399). Since the duty of sympathy is a duty of love (MM 6:452), this would seem to imply that there is a kind of sympathy which is a condition of receptiveness to the concept of duty, and that is of course what this Element claims rational sympathy to be. If we take the *Metaphysics of Morals* to provide Kant's most complete account of how the moral law is manifested in feeling, then we should think that respect is *not* the unique manifestation of lawful willing in feeling, and that sympathy is another manifestation.[37]

---

[37] It must be acknowledged that the *Metaphysics of Morals* is differently oriented to human nature than the early critical ethics. At MM 6:217, Kant says that "we shall often have to take as our

We can compare the moral-psychological dynamics of rational sympathy and respect to develop more detailed evidence for regarding rational sympathy as a moral incentive alongside respect. In Book 1, Chapter III of the *Critique of Practical Reason,* "On the incentives of pure practical reason," Kant uses a variety of terms for the changes wrought in our feelings by respect for law. It "infringes" on pathological inclinations to restrict self-love to the "condition of agreement with . . . law" (CPrR 5:73), and it thereby "deprives self-love of its influence" (5:74). It also "weakens," "humiliates," and "*strikes down*" what Kant calls "self-conceit," which is the disposition to make "claims to esteem for oneself that precede accord with the moral law" (5:73). This "thwarting" of our inclinations produces "a feeling that can be called pain" (ibid.). But along with this pain, the rational activity manifested in respect for law produces a kind of pleasure Kant calls "*self-approbation* with reference to pure practical reason" (5:80, also see 5:116) – a kind of self-esteem based not on self-conceit but on one's activity as a rational being.

As we have seen, rational sympathy involves parallel moral-psychological dynamics. It infringes on our feelings by moderating sympathetic affects that make it hard to reason and by blocking sympathetic feelings that dispose us to act wrongly. It makes sense to see this as *restricting* sympathy to the condition of agreement with law, and as *thwarting* sympathetic feelings in ways that may cause pain. We also create *new* pains and pleasures when we actively put ourselves in others' places to sympathize, or we correct existing sympathies by reasoning with others in sympathetic communication. The fact that rational sympathy involves free, rational transformations of feelings that parallel the transformations in respect for law is a reason to recognize it as a moral incentive on the same footing with respect for law.

---

object the particular *nature* of human beings, which is cognized only by experience," which indicates that he is more concerned with specific features of *human* rational nature here than he is in the earlier books: the *Groundwork*'s main focus is on "rational beings as such" (4:111), and the *Critique of Practical Reason* has no "special reference to human nature" (5:8). In the *Metaphysics of Morals*, Kant clearly focuses in greater detail on applying the moral law to the human condition. But just as clearly, he is continuing to develop his a priori moral theory in the later book. Kant gives no suggestion that the ideas in MM 6:399 are infused with empirical psychology in a way that undercuts their relevance for the kind of moral psychology Kant is doing in the earlier books. The identical language Kant uses to describe the transcendental status of respect in the second *Critique* and the broader range of feelings in the *Metaphysics of Morals* provides strong evidence that Kant is working at the same level of transcendental analysis in both places. In the *Critique of Practical Reason*, Kant describes respect as a "feeling that is not of empirical origin [*nicht empirischen Ursprungs*]" (CPrR 5:73). In the *Metaphysics of Morals*, Kant describes all the feelings on the longer list in a similar way: "Consciousness of them is not of empirical origin [*nicht empirischen Ursprungs*]; it can, instead, only follow from the consciousness of a moral law, as the effect this has on the mind" (MM 6:399).

Exclusionists, who hold that sympathy should *not* be seen as a moral incentive along with respect, may concede that the moral-psychological parallels show that there *is* a moral incentive involved in rational sympathy, but may claim that the parallels give us reason to think that rational sympathy really *just is* respect for law as applied to sympathetic feelings – rational sympathy is simply how the feeling of respect *manifests* when it happens among our sympathetic feelings.

Taken at face value, this objection conflates a particular feeling with the activity of the rational will. As explained above, Kant makes it clear that the feeling of respect *itself* is not a moral incentive – it can only be understood as such insofar as it is *seen as a manifestation* of rational activity. Thus supposing that the feeling of respect could appear in the feeling of rational sympathy would be supposing that a feeling which must *itself* be thought as appearance could appear in a *different* feeling, and this would be a category error. Further, it should be abundantly clear that respect and rational sympathy *feel different*, despite their dynamical commonalities. Respect for law is a dialectic of humiliation and self-approbation of the "subject toward his master," even though "the master lies in us" (Rel 6:23). The moments in rational sympathy where we moderate affect and block sympathy that disposes us to act wrongly may involve similar humiliation and self-approbation, and perhaps we *can* call these moments respect for law. But these are only *some* of the moments in rational sympathy. Freely stepping into others' places, and communicating with them to correct our sympathies, has nothing to do with humiliation before a master or self-approbation. It is a dialectic of caring communication with finite others who stand with us as moral peers upon the same moral plane.

Exclusionists may reply that their claim is not that the *feeling* of respect is manifested in rational sympathy, but that the same *rational activity* manifested in respect is manifested in rational sympathy. Now, if reason is a unity (A302/B359; G 4:391), then it is always the same reason which is active. At a high enough level of transcendental analysis, it makes sense to assume that the rational activity manifested in the feelings of respect and rational sympathy is a single kind of activity, a kind of activity in which moral agents freely act in ways that regulate and transform their feelings. Exclusionists might claim that the activity we identify at this level of analysis is better understood in terms of respect than in terms of sympathy, but it is hard to see how such a claim could be made without another conflation of activity and manifestation. Further, there are clearly differences in how the activity proceeds in respect for law and sympathy. This can be seen in the different moral *objects* of these feelings. We can say that respect for law has *no* object, or that it takes the *form* of law itself as its object: Respect "depends on the representation of a law only as to its form and not on account of any object of the law" (CPrR 5:79).[38] It is a feeling about commands involving absolute prohibitions and mandates. The moral objects of rational sympathy are finite others in their particularity, and the elements of their happiness – their merely permissible ends – and it is a feeling about freely incorporating these ends into our own wills.[39]

14 Contemporary and Historical Connections to Empathy

It is intuitive to suppose that rational sympathy is not just a fanciful theoretical construct but a capacity we actually have, and that perspective-taking and feeling-sharing of the forms described here are parts of our everyday moral experience. We can also find evidence in contemporary empirical psychology that this is the case, in discussions of *empathy*. There is no generally accepted distinction between sympathy and empathy (Stueber 2006: 27), and some theorists characterize them in ways that make them overlapping phenomena. Ideas in contemporary and historical empathy theory cast useful light on Kant's theory of sympathy. Kant's distinction between rational sympathy (on the one hand) and episodes of natural sympathy which prompt affect (on the other) corresponds closely and is plausibly identical to a distinction drawn in contemporary empirical psychology between *empathic concern* and *empathic distress* (Tangney 1991: 599).[40]

Empathic concern involves "feelings of compassion and warmth felt for the target of empathy" (Hodges et al. 2007: 390). It is an "intentional capacity" which involves "emotion regulation" – it "involves an explicit representation of

---

[38] Kant says that respect can be directed to persons (5:76) but that this is strictly speaking respect for the law that their examples hold before us (5:78). We might say that respect for persons is a feeling for the moral significance of their universal and necessary features as rational agents, while sympathy is a feeling for the moral significance of what is particular and contingent about them as individual human beings.

[39] Some might suppose that respect for law is something human beings must share with all sensibly conditioned rational beings, but rational sympathy is not. As interpreted in this book, however, rational sympathy is necessary for human beings because of features Kant seems to think we share with all sensibly conditioned rational beings. Kant seems to think all such beings have contingent sensibilities and duties to adopt others' ends, and are governed by the same a priori principles of intentional teleology. If this is right, then not only human beings but all sensibly conditioned rational beings must rationally sympathize to adopt others' MPEs.

[40] There are no doubt other connections worth exploring between Kant's theory of sympathy and contemporary empirical psychology – I focus on this connection because of its centrality for the themes of the book. Other ideas discussed in section 5 may have contemporary connections. For example, Kant's notion of a merely "logical" and "heuristic" way of putting ourselves in others' places which does not necessarily prompt sympathetic feelings may connect with what is sometimes called "cognitive empathy" in the contemporary context (e.g. Blair 2007: 4–5). Kant's idea that the inclinations of those in a "distinguished" class dispose them to narrow sympathies for the "humble" may connect with work on the hazards of group empathy (e.g. Sirin et al. 2017). Kant's view that we can put ourselves into the position of *everyone* (section 5) may connect with work on ways to make group empathy more universal (e.g. Levine et al. 2005).

the subjectivity of the other" rather than "a simple resonance of affect between the self and other" (Decety et al. 2007: 254). *Empathic distress*, by contrast, is a feeling which Decety et al. (ibid.) call "emotional contagion." Hodges et al. (2007: 402) say that it "occurs when people fail to rein in emotional empathy," and note that "[t]he quintessential example of this phenomenon is the bystander who witnesses a gruesome accident and can only stand by, gasping and shrieking, rather than comforting the victim or going for help."

Psychologists think that it is the development of regulatory processes which allows us to feel empathic concern rather than empathic distress. While it appears that some of this regulation is unconscious, there is evidence that conscious perspective-taking plays a role in this regulation too. Asking people to "imagine things from the empathy target's point of view consistently increases empathic concern" (Hodges et al. 2007: 393; also see Batson et al. 1997). On the other hand, imagining things from the other's perspective *too* vividly can prompt empathic distress, and we can modify *how* we frame our engagement with the other's position to moderate our empathic feelings. Hodges et al. note that therapists are sometimes "trained to restate the client's feelings from the client's perspective ('So, you're feeling betrayed by your mother's actions') rather than putting themselves in the place of the client (e.g. 'If my mother did that to me, I'd feel so betrayed!')" (Hodges et al. 2007: 393). This implies that voluntarily exercising the skill of perspective-taking can serve both to prompt and also moderate feeling.

These remarks from contemporary discussions of empathy show that there is a close correspondence between empathic concern and rational sympathy, as well as a close correspondence between empathic distress and episodes of natural sympathy which prompt affect. This raises two interesting questions. The first is a question about translation, and the second is a question about the history of the concept of empathy.

First, do these connections suggest that we ought to use the term "empathy" instead of "sympathy" to translate Kant if we want to produce translations that engage as closely as possible with contemporary thought? Given that Kant uses *Sympathie* in many of the texts we have seen, and that it is obviously a very close cognate of "sympathy," it would do violence to the texts to replace "sympathy" with "empathy." But there is at least one use in Kant's corpus of a very close cognate of "empathy," that is, "*empathie*." It appears in the Vigilantius Ethics, in a contrast with apathy: Kant describes "apathy [*apathie*]" as "the renunciation of all affects^t [*affecte*]," and "empathy [*empathie*]" as "the passionate abandonment of the soul to all of them" (Eth-V 27:662). Here the Cambridge translation (by Peter Heath) uses "empathy." Kant uses other language that is reasonably translated with "empathy." Consider Anth-F 25:476, a passage discussed earlier: "*Im moralischen Beurtheilen, ist das Vermögen nöthig sein Ich zu versetzen, und sich in den Stand Punckt und die Stelle des andern zu setzen, so daß man mit ihm denckt, und sich in ihm fühlt*" (Anth-F 25:476). Kant's expression "*so daß man mit ihm denckt, und sich in ihm fühlt*" is literally "so that one thinks with him, and feels in him." Thus Cambridge translator G. Felicitas Munzel quite reasonably translates this phrase as "so that one thinks with him, and has empathy with him" (Anth-F 25:476). I replaced Munzel's "empathy" with "sympathy" when I quoted this passage earlier, to maintain consistency with the discussion, and more importantly, because the evidence adduced in this Element suggests that Kant's concept of sympathy is sophisticated enough to capture what some contemporary psychologists mean by "empathy." This suggests that we could not usefully try to attribute to Kant any systematic distinction between sympathy and empathy without textual evidence of a kind that simply does not appear in Kant's corpus.

One more passage which evokes the concept psychologists seem to have in mind with "empathy" is worth noting because of its connection with the question about the history of the concept of empathy to be discussed next. According to Herder's Ethics notes, Kant claims that in "true sympathy [*wahrhaftigen Sympathie*]" with another, "we really feel ourselves^t in his place" [*wir uns wirklich in seiner Stelle fühlen*]" (Eth-H 27:58). This characterization would seem to fit the model of empathy used by the psychologists quoted above just as well as it fits true sympathy for Kant.

This point about Herder's notes is philosophically peripheral for understanding Kant if Kant does not systematically distinguish sympathy and empathy. But it may nonetheless be historically significant for the concept of empathy. According to an influential history by Lauren Wispé, "the concept we know today as empathy began as *Einfühlung* [literally "feeling into"] in late nineteenth-century German aesthetics and was translated as empathy in early twentieth-century American experimental psychology" (1987: 17). This no doubt captures an important episode in the history of this concept. However, the evidence we have seen implies that the history extends earlier. Karsten Stueber gives a history which extends into German romanticism, citing a 1774 text from Herder as the earliest point in his history. According to Stueber, "in his 'Vom Erkennen und Empfinden der menschlichen Seele' [1774], Herder ... speaks of the ability of humankind 'to feel into everything, to feel everything out of himself' ... (1774 (1964), 7–8)" (Stueber's translation, Stueber 2006: 6). In this passage, Herder has in mind a notion of empathy panpsychically extended into the world beyond the realm of the human. We find a notion of empathy much more like the one addressed in contemporary empirical psychology in the passage from Herder's notes from Kant's Ethics class just quoted. We know that Herder's notes date from 1772–1774, so it is reasonable to think that Herder's thoughts in his 1774 publication were at least partly developments of, or responses to, Kant's remarks. This would seem to imply that if Herder played a significant role in originating the concept of empathy, then Kant did too. The thought that Kant may have played a significant role in originating the concept of empathy turns on its head the picture of Kant often formed by readers who are only exposed to Kant's seemingly dismissive attitude toward sharing feelings in the *Groundwork* and second *Critique*.

15 Conclusion

This Element has sought to contribute to an inclusive reading of Kantian sympathy, according to which sympathy can be understood as an activity of the autonomous will and a moral incentive on the same footing with respect for law. It argues that Kant endorses a distinction between rational and natural sympathy which is essential for his moral theory. These two ways of sympathizing can involve qualitatively identical sympathetic joys and sorrows but are differently oriented to practical reason. Rational sympathy is active and regulated by practical reason, and is necessary for us to actively fulfill our duty to adopt others' MPEs as our own. Natural sympathy is passive and driven by inclination, and while it can contingently allow us to fulfill our duty to adopt others' MPEs, it can also prompt affect and dispose us to act wrongly.

Rational and natural sympathy are both functions of the a posteriori imagination. In both kinds of sympathy, the a posteriori imagination subjectively synthesizes an imaginary version of the first-person vantage point of the person with whom I sympathize. This imaginary subjective synthesis provides the *form* of sympathy. The sensible *content* which furnishes this form is provided by the imagination's power to associate sensible representations with concepts, a power that Kant explains in his third *Critique* discussion of aesthetic ideas. The person with whom I sympathize communicates concepts to me, and I imaginatively associate sensible content with those concepts which is drawn from *my* past experience, but which I creatively transform and use to constitute an imaginary version of *her* experience. I have sympathetic feelings in response to this imagined experience. In natural sympathy, I find myself passively driven into this imaginary standpoint by my inclinations, and I passively furnish it with sensible content via inclination-driven associations with the concepts the other shares. In rational sympathy, I actively place myself in it, and carefully associate the sensible content that I think will help me sympathize correctly.

Kant thinks can know a priori that we can sympathize correctly about beauty, sublimity, and morality, but we cannot know a priori that we can sympathize correctly about feelings that are contingent from the perspective of practical rationality. However, both Kant and common sense tell us that we do often sympathize correctly about contingent feelings. This means we can come to know that our sympathy about contingent feelings is correct a posteriori, through communication, and trial and error. If sympathy is necessary to fulfill the imperfect duty to adopt others' MPEs, then it is not a moral liability if our capacity to sympathize is imperfect.

Sympathy is necessary to adopt others' MPEs because others' MPEs are individuated in terms of their own concepts of their MPEs. Others' concepts of their MPEs often (and perhaps always) contain marks of the first person, and should contain no marks of law apart from permissibility. Sympathy allows me to adopt ends individuated with concepts with marks of the first person because sympathy allows me to imaginatively step into others' first-person perspectives. Sympathy is necessary for me to adopt another's end when it is individuated with a concept whose only mark of law is permissibility because permissibility does not sufficiently determine an end for me to pursue it out of respect for law. All rational agents can pursue obligatory or meritorious ends out of respect for law, because they can be motivated by feelings about law which are necessary for rational agents to have. But we ought not to include marks of obligation or merit in the concepts individuating our MPEs. If I am to adopt others' MPEs in terms of their concepts, I must make their concepts of their MPEs get purchase on my contingent feelings. I can only do this if I can freely make my contingent feelings sympathetically correspond to their feelings.

Rational sympathy solves a puzzle in Kant's theory of friendship. The Kantian sage can appear to reject sympathetic suffering when she cannot help a suffering friend. The theory of rational sympathy shows that this appearance is mistaken. Sages as well as ordinary people should suffer with friends even when they cannot help, because sympathy is necessary to fulfill the imperfect duty to adopt friends' MPEs, and we ought to take friends' MPEs as our own.

At the risk of asking too much of readers' corresponding feelings, I will close with a metaphor. Some scholars may see one of the ideas I have argued against, that respect for law suffices for taking others' ends as our own, as essential to the sublimity of Kantian moral rationalism. But we can find the abstract height of the moral law sublime, and still see its roots and branches as extending deeply and broadly into the particularity and diversity of our feelings and our relationships with others. Kant's theory of rational sympathy shows us how to see it this way. The rational form of the kingdom of ends includes not only the sublime, monochromatic skeleton of stern respect, but also all the joyful and sorrowful feelings we share with one another in rational sympathy.

Abbreviations

Abbreviations and translations for Kant's texts are as follows, unless otherwise noted. "ᵗ" within quoted passages indicates my modifications of translations. Except for A/B, pagination is by *Akademie* edition, unless otherwise noted. "NA" at the end of entries in the list below indicates texts not included in the Akademie edition; references to these are paginated according to the volume cited.

A/B: *Critique of Pure Reason* (Kant 1998).

Anth: *Anthropology from a Pragmatic Point of View*, trans. Robert B. Louden in Kant 2007: 231–429.

Anth-F: Friedländer notes from Kant's Anthropology lectures, trans. G. Felicitas Munzel in Kant 2012: 37–255.

Anth-Mr: Mrongovius notes from Kant's Anthropology lectures, trans. Robert R. Clewis in Kant 2012: 335–509.

CPrR: *Critique of Practical Reason*, in Kant 1996a: 137–271.

CPJ: *Critique of the Power of Judgment* (Kant 2000).

Eth-B: Brauer notes from Kant's Ethics lectures, in Kant 1924[NA].

Eth-C: Collins notes from Kant's Ethics lectures, in Kant 1997a: 37–222.

Eth-H: Herder notes from Kant's Ethics lectures, in Kant 1997a: 1–36.

Eth-Mr: Mrongovius notes from Kant's Ethics lectures, in Kant 1979: 1395–1581.

Eth-V: Vigilantius notes from Kant's Ethics lectures, in Kant 1997a: 249–452.

G: *Groundwork of the Metaphysics of Morals*, in Kant 1996a: 41–108.

Met-L2: L2 Metaphysics lecture notes, in Kant 1997b: 297–354.

Met-Mr: Mrongovius notes from Kant's Metaphysics lectures, in Kant 1997b: 107–286.

MM: *The Metaphysics of Morals*, in Kant 1996: 363–602.

OFBS: *Observations on the Feeling of the Beautiful and Sublime*, trans. Paul Guyer in Kant 2007: 23–62.

OP: *Opus Posthumum* (Kant 1993).

P: *Prolegomena to Any Future Metaphysics That Will Be Able to Come Forward as a Science*, trans. Gary Hatfield in Kant 2002: 49–169.

Ped: *Lectures on Pedagogy* (Kant's own lecture notes), trans. Robert B. Louden in Kant 2007: 437–485.

Rel: *Religion within the Boundaries of Mere Reason*, in Kant 1996a: 39–216.

TP: "On the Common Saying: That May Be Correct in Theory, But It Is of No Use in Practice", in Kant 1996: 273–309.

Bibliography

Kant's Texts

Kant, Immanuel (1924). *Eine Vorlesung Kants über Ethik. Im Auftrag der Kantgesellschaft herausgegeben von Paul Menzer.* Ed. Paul Menzer. Berlin-Charlottenburg: Pan Verlag Rolf Heise.

Kant, Immanuel (1979). *Kant's gesammelte Schriften: Vorlesungen über Moralphilosophie, Band 27, Hälfte 2, T1 2.* Ed. Berlin-Brandenburgische Akademie der Wissenschaften. Berlin: Walter de Gruyter.

Kant, Immanuel (1993). *Opus Posthumum.* Trans. and ed. Eckart Förster and Michael Rosen. Eckart Förster. Cambridge: Cambridge University Press.

Kant, Immanuel (1996a). *Practical Philosophy.* Trans. and ed. Mary J. Gregor. Cambridge: Cambridge University Press.

Kant, Immanuel (1996b). *Religion and Rational Theology.* Trans. and ed. Allen W. Wood and George di Giovanni. Cambridge: Cambridge University Press.

Kant, Immanuel (1997a). *Lectures on Ethics.* Trans. Peter Heath, ed. Peter Heath and J. B. Schneewind. Cambridge: Cambridge University Press.

Kant, Immanuel (1997b). *Lectures on Metaphysics.* Trans. and ed. Karl Ameriks and Steve Naragon. Cambridge: Cambridge University Press.

Kant, Immanuel (1998). *Critique of Pure Reason.* Trans. and ed. Paul Guyer and Allen W. Wood. Cambridge: Cambridge University Press.

Kant, Immanuel (2000). *Critique of the Power of Judgment.* Trans. Paul Guyer and Eric Matthews, ed. Paul Guyer. Cambridge: Cambridge University Press.

Kant, Immanuel (2002). *Theoretical Philosophy after 1781.* Ed. Henry Allison and Peter Heath. Cambridge: Cambridge University Press

Kant, Immanuel (2007). *Anthropology, History and Education.* Ed. Günther Zöller and Robert B. Louden. Cambridge: Cambridge University Press.

Kant, Immanuel (2012). *Lectures on Anthropology.* Ed. Allen W. Wood and Robert B. Louden. Cambridge: Cambridge University Press.

Other Sources

Baron, M. (1995). *Kantian Ethics Almost without Apology.* Ithaca: Cornell University Press.

Baron, M. (2013). "Friendship, Duties Regarding Specific Conditions of Persons, and the Virtues of Social Intercourse, (TL 6:468 – 474)." In *Kant's Tugendlehre: A Comprehensive Commentary,* eds. A. Trampota, O. Sensen, and J. Timmermann. Berlin: De Gruyter, 365–382.

Baron, M. and Fahmy, M. S. (2009). "Beneficence and Other Duties of Love." In *The Blackwell Guide to Kant's Ethics*, ed. T. E. Hill. Oxford: Wiley-Blackwell, 211–228.

Batson, C. D., Early, S., and Salvarani, G. (1997). "Perspective Taking: Imagining How Another Feels versus Imagining How You Would Feel." *Personality and Social Psychology Bulletin* 23, 751–758.

Baxley, A. M. (2010). *Kant's Theory of Virtue: The Value of Autocracy*. New York: Cambridge University Press.

Blair, R. J. R. (2007). "The Cognitive Neuropsychology of Empathy." In *Empathy and Mental Illness*, eds. T. F. D. Farrow and P. W. R. Woodruff. Cambridge: Cambridge University Press, 3–16.

Cohen, A. (2008). "The Ultimate Kantian Experience: Kant on Dinner Parties." *History of Philosophy Quarterly* 25 (4), 315–336.

Decety, J., Jackson, P. L., and Brunet, E. (2007). "The Cognitive Neuropsychology of Empathy." In *Empathy and Mental Illness*, eds. T. F. D. Farrow and P. W. R. Woodruff. Cambridge: Cambridge University Press, 240–260.

Denis, L. (2000). "Kant's Cold Sage and the Sublimity of Apathy." *Kantian Review* 4 (1), 48–73.

Fahmy, M. S. (2009). "Active Sympathetic Participation: Reconsidering Kant's Duty of Sympathy." *Kantian Review* 14 (1), 31–52.

Fahmy, M. S. (2010). "Kantian Practical Love." *Pacific Philosophical Quarterly* 91 (3), 313–331.

Fahmy, M. S. (2016). "Love's Reasons." *Journal of Value Inquiry* 50, 153–168.

Fahmy, M. S. (2019). "On Virtues of Love and Wide Ethical Duties." *Kantian Review* 24 (3), 415–437.

Guyer, P. (2010). "Moral Feelings in the *Metaphysics of Morals*." In *Kant's Metaphysics of Morals: A Critical Guide*, ed. L. Denis. New York: Cambridge University Press, 130–151.

Hay, C. (2013). *Kantianism, Liberalism, and Feminism: Resisting Oppression*. New York: Palgrave-Macmillan.

Herder, J. (1964/1774). "Vom Erkennen und Empfinden der menschlichen Seele." In *Herders Werke*, vol. 3., ed. W. Dobbek. Berlin: Aufbau Verlag, 7–69.

Herman, B. (1993). *The Practice of Moral Judgment*. Cambridge, MA: Harvard University Press.

Hildebrand, C. (2023). "Feeling, Cognition, and the Eighteenth-Century Context of Kantian Sympathy." *British Journal for the History of Philosophy* 31 (5), 974–1004.

Hodges, S. D. and Biswas-Diener, R. (2007). "Balancing the Empathy Expense Account: Strategies for Regulating Empathic Response." In *Empathy and*

Mental Illness, eds. T. F. D. Farrow and P. W. R. Woodruff. Cambridge: Cambridge University Press, 390–407.

Hurter, S., Paloyelis, Y., Williams, A., and Fotopoulou, A. (2014). "Partners' Empathy Increases Pain Ratings: Effects of Perceived Empathy and Attachment Style on Pain Report and Display." *The Journal of Pain* 15 (9), 934–944.

Korsgaard, C. (1996). *Creating the Kingdom of Ends*. Cambridge: Cambridge University Press.

Levine, M., Prosser, A., Evans, D., and Reicher, S. (2005). "Identity and Emergency Intervention: How Social Group Membership and Inclusiveness of Group Boundaries Shape Helping Behavior." *Personality and Social Psychology Bulletin* 31 (4), 443–453.

Makkreel, R. A. (2012). "Relating Aesthetic and Sociable Feelings to Moral and Participatory Feelings: Reassessing Kant on Sympathy and Honor." In *Kant's Observations and Remarks: A Critical Guide*, eds. S. M. Shell and R. Velkley. Cambridge: Cambridge University Press, 101–115.

Miller, S. C. (2012). *The Ethics of Need: Agency, Dignity, and Obligation*. New York: Routledge.

Paton, H. J. (1948). *The Categorical Imperative: A Study in Kant's Moral Philosophy*. Chicago: University of Chicago Press.

Paton, H. J. (1956). "Kant on Friendship." *Proceedings of the British Academy* 42, 45–66.

Paytas, T. (2015). "Rational Beings with Emotional Needs: The Patient-Centered Grounds of Kant's Duty of Humanity." *History of Philosophy Quarterly* 32 (4), 353–376.

Sherman, N. (1997). *Making a Necessity of Virtue: Aristotle and Kant on Virtue*. Cambridge: Cambridge University Press.

Sirin, C., Valentino, N., and Villalobos, J. D. (2017). "The Social Causes and Political Consequences of Group Empathy." *Political Psychology* 38 (3), 427–448.

Stueber, K. (2006). *Rediscovering Empathy: Agency, Folk Psychology, and the Human Sciences*. Cambridge, MA: MIT Press.

Tangney, J. P. (1991). "Moral Affect: The Good, the Bad, and the Ugly." *Journal of Personality and Social Psychology* 61, 598–607.

Thomason, K. (2017). "A Good Enough Heart: Kant and the Cultivation of Emotions." *Kantian Review* 22 (3), 441–462.

Timmermann, J. (2014). "Kant and the Second-Person Standpoint." *Grazer Philosophische Studien* 90, 131–147.

Timmermann, J. (2016). "Kant über Mitleidenschaft." *Kant-Studien* 107 (4), 729–732.

Timmermann, J. (n.d.). *Kant's Theory of Sympathy*. Book manuscript.

Varden, H. (2020a). *Sex, Love, and Gender: A Kantian Theory*. Oxford: Oxford University Press.

Varden, H. (2020b). "Kantian Care." In *Caring for Liberalism: Dependency and Political Theory*, eds. A. Baehr and A. Bhandary. New York: Routledge, 50–74.

Vilhauer, B. (2021a). "'Reason's Sympathy' and Its Foundations in Productive Imagination." *Kantian Review* 26 (3), 455–474.

Vilhauer, B. (2021b). "Sages, Sympathy, and Suffering in Kant's Theory of Friendship." *Canadian Journal of Philosophy* 51 (6), 452–467.

Vilhauer, B. (2022). "'Reason's Sympathy' and Others' Ends in Kant." *European Journal of Philosophy* 30 (1), 96–112.

Wispé, L. (1987). "History of the Concept of Empathy." In *Empathy and Its Development*, eds. N. Eisenberg and J. Strayer. Cambridge: Cambridge University Press, 17–37.

Wood, A. W. (1999). *Kant's Ethical Thought*. New York: Cambridge University Press.

Wood, A. W. (2008). *Kantian Ethics*. New York: Cambridge University Press.

Acknowledgments

Thanks to my parents Susan and Jon, my wife Ruvanee, my son Kian, my brother Tom, and my old friends Mark Marasco and Jerry Brown, for abundant data on the value of particular relationships. Thanks also to friends as well as occasional but indispensable interlocutors in academia who shared helpful communications at various points. Special thanks to Matthew Altman, Melissa Seymour Fahmy, and Owen Ware for detailed comments. Thanks also to Jeffrey Blustein, Alix Cohen, Lara Denis, Corey Dyck, Jonathan Gilmore, Robert Hartman, Anne Kornhauser, Colin Marshall, Derk Pereboom, Eric Steinhart, Thomas Teufel, Jens Timmermann, Allen Wood, Rachel Zuckert, and the editors and reviewers at Cambridge and the journals that published the papers upon which this Element draws.

Cambridge Elements

The Philosophy of Immanuel Kant

Desmond Hogan
Princeton University

Desmond Hogan joined the philosophy department at Princeton in 2004. His interests include Kant, Leibniz and German rationalism, early modern philosophy, and questions about causation and freedom. Recent work includes 'Kant on the Foreknowledge of Contingent Truths', *Res Philosophica* 91 (1) (2014); 'Kant's Theory of Divine and Secondary Causation', in Brandon Look (ed.) *Leibniz and Kant*, Oxford University Press (2021); 'Kant and the Character of Mathematical Inference', in Carl Posy and Ofra Rechter (eds.) *Kant's Philosophy of Mathematics Vol. I*, Cambridge University Press (2020).

Howard Williams
University of Cardiff

Howard Williams was appointed Honorary Distinguished Professor at the Department of Politics and International Relations, University of Cardiff in 2014. He is also Emeritus Professor in Political Theory at the Department of International Politics, Aberystwyth University, a member of the Coleg Cymraeg Cenedlaethol (Welsh-language national college) and a Fellow of the Learned Society of Wales. He is the author of *Marx* (1980); *Kant's Political Philosophy* (1983); *Concepts of Ideology* (1988); *Hegel, Heraclitus and Marx's Dialectic* (1989); *International Relations in Political Theory* (1992); *International Relations and the Limits of Political Theory* (1996); *Kant's Critique of Hobbes: Sovereignty and Cosmopolitanism* (2003); *Kant and the End of War* (2012) and is currently editor of the journal Kantian Review. He is writing a book on the Kantian legacy in political philosophy for a new series edited by Paul Guyer.

Allen Wood
Indiana University

Allen Wood is Ward W. and Priscilla B. Woods Professor Emeritus at Stanford University. He was a John S. Guggenheim Fellow at the Free University in Berlin, a National Endowment for the Humanities Fellow at the University of Bonn and Isaiah Berlin Visiting Professor at the University of Oxford. He is on the editorial board of eight philosophy journals, five book series and The Stanford Encyclopedia of Philosophy. Along with Paul Guyer, Professor Wood is co-editor of The Cambridge Edition of the Works of Immanuel Kant and translator of the Critique of Pure Reason. He is the author or editor of a number of other works, mainly on Kant, Hegel and Karl Marx. His most recently published books are *Fichte's Ethical Thought*, Oxford University Press (2016) and *Kant and Religion*, Cambridge University Press (2020). Wood is a member of the American Academy of Arts and Sciences.

About the Series

This Cambridge Elements series provides an extensive overview of Kant's philosophy and its impact upon philosophy and philosophers. Distinguished Kant specialists provide an up-to-date summary of the results of current research in their fields and give their own take on what they believe are the most significant debates influencing research, drawing original conclusions.

Cambridge Elements ≡

The Philosophy of Immanuel Kant

Elements in the Series

Anthropology from a Kantian Point of View
Robert B. Louden

Introducing Kant's Critique of Pure Reason
Paul Guyer and Allen Wood

Kant's Theory of Conscience
Samuel Kahn

Rationalizing (Vernünfteln *)*
Martin Sticker

Kant and the French Revolution
Reidar Maliks

The Kantian Federation
Luigi Caranti

The Politics of Beauty: A Study of Kant's Critique of Taste
Susan Meld Shell

Kant's Theory of Labour
Jordan Pascoe

Kant's Late Philosophy of Nature: The Opus postumum
Stephen Howard

Kant on Freedom
Owen Ware

Kant on Self-Control
Marijana Vujošević

Kant on Rational Sympathy
Benjamin Vilhauer

A full series listing is available at: www.cambridge.org/EPIK